PATTERN MAGIC 2

Tomoko Nakamichi

Laurence King Publishing

LAURENCE KING

Published in 2011 by Laurence King Publishing Ltd
361–373 City Road
London EC1V 1LR
United Kingdom
Tel: + 44 20 7841 6900
Fax: + 44 20 7841 6910
e-mail: enquiries@laurenceking.com
www.laurenceking.com

Pattern Magic 2 by Tomoko Nakamichi
Copyright © Tomoko Nakamichi 2007
Original Japanese edition published by Bunka Publishing Bureau, Bunka Gakuen
Educational Foundation.

This English edition is published by arrangement with Bunka Publishing Bureau, Bunka
Gakuen Educational Foundation, Tokyo, by means of Tuttle-Mori Agency, Inc., Tokyo.

Tomoko Nakamichi has asserted her right under the Copyright, Designs, and Patent
Act 1988, to be identified as the Author of this Work.

A catalogue record for this book is available from the British Library.

ISBN: 978-1-85669-706-4

Photographer: Masaaki Kawade
Original design and layout: Tomoko Yamaguchi-Yama

English edition design: Mark Holt
Typeface: Sabon and Syntax
Senior Editor: Sophie Page
Printed in China

Tomoko Nakamichi

Having served many years as a professor at Bunka Fashion College,
Tomoko Nakamichi currently delivers lectures and holds courses on
pattern making, both in her native Japan and internationally. This book
brings together the results of the research on garment patterns she has
carried out to help instruct her students. She also enjoys creating the ball-
jointed fashion dolls that appear in the pages of this book.

Garments we design ourselves appeal to the emotions

as well as the eye.

Unexpected shapes and forms can be converted into flat

patterns and ultimately into garments. From this new ideas

develop, making the process a rewarding one.

I want to copy forms and details that I create unexpectedly

onto a flat surface to understand their structure as a pattern.

Patterns are like documents that describe a garment,

conveying its structure more eloquently than words.

They can even convey the thoughts of its creator.

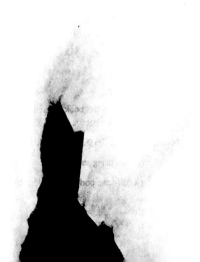

Contents

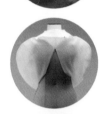

The dress form used in this book is based on the standard Bunka-style sloper (block) for an adult Japanese female. See page 100 for more details.

All patterns are for a size [...] ult female (bust 83cm, waist 64cm, centre back length 38cm).

The position of the cutting [...] ut lines, and the amount to be opened out may vary according to garment size.

When using a half-scale b[...] [...]duce to half all full-sized measurements and develop the pattern.

Part 2
Decorative structures

Part 3
It vanished …

Using this book

A major objective when making garments for women is not only that they fit properly but also that they look attractive. For this reason, garment design will always be important and fulfilling. I hope the pattern-making method I introduce here is of use to you in turning an image into a silhouette or design detail, and that you learn from the ideas in this book and then find new methods that work for you.

The pattern drafting and manipulation for the design of garments in this book are based on the Bunka-style sloper (block) for adult women (Japanese 'M' size: bust 83cm, waist 64cm, centre back length 38cm), and a half-scale dress form for the three-dimensional pattern manipulation. All the measurements on this dress form are half those of a full-sized dress form; its surface area is scaled down to a quarter and its volume to one-eighth. Using a half-scale dress form helps you to understand better the overall balance and look of a garment. As my objective was to explain the construction of a pattern in an easy-to-follow way, I have omitted pattern markings such as the facing lines used for actually constructing the garment and the amount of fabric required to make the garment.

Abbreviations used in pattern drafting

BP
Bust Point

AH
Arm Hole

FAH
Front Arm Hole

BAH
Back Arm Hole

B
Bust

W
Waist

MH
Mid Hip

H
Hip

BL
Bust Line

WL
Waist Line

HL
Hip Line

EL
Elbow Line

CF
Centre Front

CB
Centre Back

Symbols used in pattern drafting

Guide line	——————————	Line that acts as a guide when drawing other lines. Shown by a thin solid line.
Sector line	⌒⌒	Line indicating that one line of a fixed length has been divided into equal lengths. Shown by a thin broken line.
Finishing line	▬▬▬▬	Line indicating the finished outline of a pattern. Shown by a thick solid line or a broken line.
Cut on the fold	▬ ▬ ▬ ▬	Line indicating where the fabric is to be cut on the fold. Shown by a thick broken line.
Top stitching line	- - - - - - - - -	Line indicating the position of the top stitching. Shown by a thin broken line.
Gathers	∿∿∿∿∿	Line indicating the position where gathers are to be inserted. Shown by a thin solid line.
Facing line	—·—·—·—	Line indicating the position and size of a facing. Shown by a thick dot-dash line.
Right angle marking		Indicates a right angle. Shown by a thin solid line.
Marking to indicate intersections of lines		Indicates that the left and right lines intersect.
Grain line	←———→	Indicates that the cross-wise grain of the fabric runs in the direction of the arrows. Shown by a thick solid line.
Bias direction	↗	Indicates the direction of the bias of the fabric. Shown by a thick solid line.
Extension marking	←⌒→	Indicates the part to be stretched.
Ease marking	⤙⌒⤚	Indicates the part to be eased.
Close and cut open marking	Close Open	Indicates that the paper pattern is to be folded along the dotted lines and cut open along the solid line.
Marking to cut fabric with paper pattern pieces arranged contiguously		Indicates that the paper pattern pieces are to be arranged contiguously when cutting out the fabric.

Fundamentals

Create three-dimensional forms with design lines only

The Bunka-style sloper (block) used as the base for pattern-making is fitted to the body with darts (bust darts, back shoulder darts, waist darts). The first chapter explains how to create a three-dimensional form, not with darts, but with design lines inserted freely into the pattern of a basic torso.

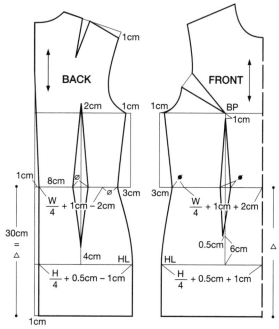

❶ Draft the pattern for the torso.

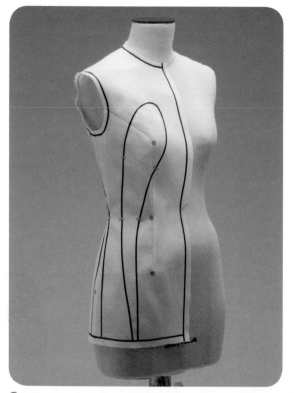

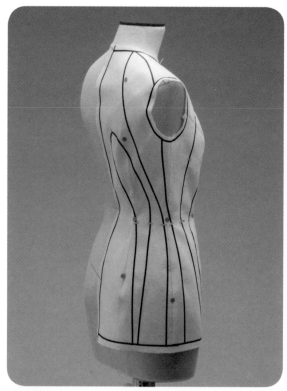

❷ Finish sewing the bodice and add ● markings at the end of the darts and on the waistline.
Draw lines in any way you want regardless of the position of the ● markings. Insert alignment markings for when you sew the garment together.

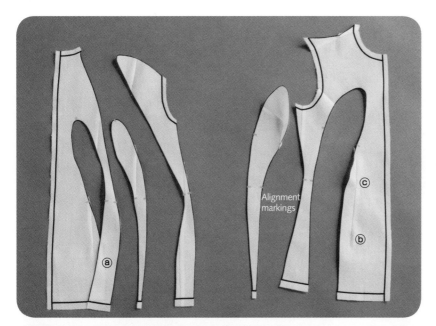

Alignment markings

ⓒ

ⓑ

❸ If you cut along the lines, the pieces do not lie uniformly flat and places at which they cross over can occur as shown by ⓐ.

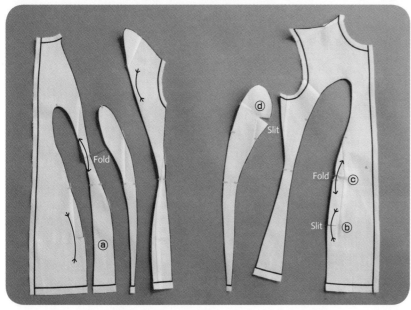

Fold

ⓐ

ⓓ

Slit

Fold

ⓒ

Slit

ⓑ

❹ By folding ⓐ, I created some seam allowance. At other points where the pattern pieces do not lie flat, as shown in ⓑ, make slits in the fabric towards the end of the darts. At points where there is excess fabric and it is rising as shown in ⓒ, fold etc. to flatten. When sewing together, stretch the places you have folded and either ease or flatten the three points where you have made slits in the fabric.

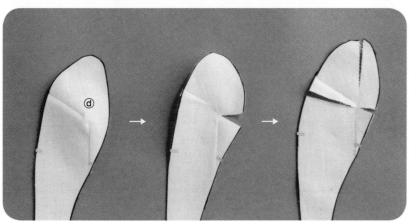

ⓓ

❺ A slit was made on piece ⓓ, but because there is a large amount for cutting and opening out, make slits in the fabric in three places and distribute the ease.

Cut piece ⓓ

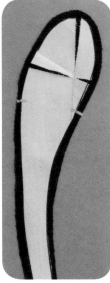

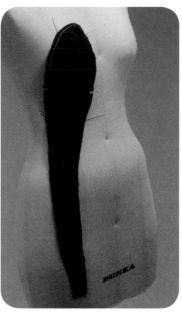

(1) Place the fabric pattern on top of the fabric, add seam allowances and cut.

(2) Do not forget to add alignment markings.

(3) Machine-stitch with a long stitch along the parts that have been cut and opened out, and ease with an iron.

(4) It fits to the chest even without darts.

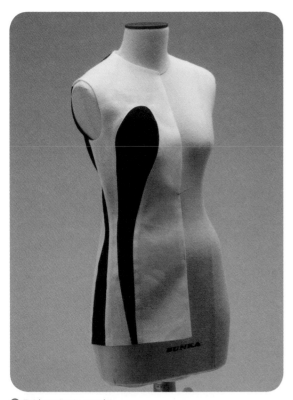

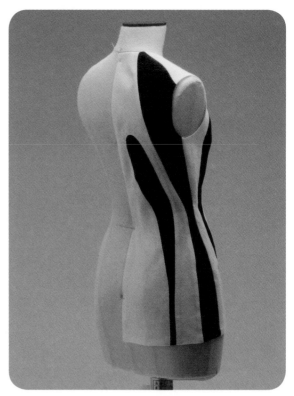

⑤ Finish sewing to complete
The further the design lines are from the ● markings, the more you will need to shape the fabric. If they are too far away, it will be impossible to shape the fabric (but that also depends on the fabric), so you may have to make changes to the design such as by increasing the number of design lines.

By way of further application, I inserted flare into the hem

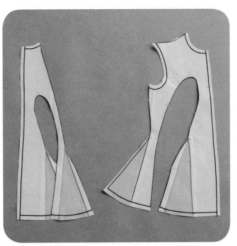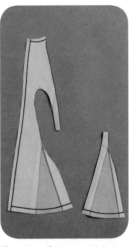

1 Using the pattern in **4**, draw lines where you want to insert flare.

2 Cut and open out the amount for the flare. Here, flare has been inserted in the side seam of the bodice front. The panels on the bodice back overlap and a one-piece pattern is not possible. As they overlap to a large degree, seam allowance cannot be created by folding the top. Change the design by dividing the pattern into two pieces.

The pattern that was cut into two pieces.

3 Finish sewing to complete
Depending on the way you insert the design lines, various changes to the pattern will be required. Always be flexible in your thinking as you find ways to complete your garment.

Part 1
Playing with geometrics

Since I first began studying mathematics,

I have always loved the circle.

More than any other shape,

there is a simplicity about it.

I began making patterns for garments,

starting with the circle,

then the triangle and the square …

When you wrap these shapes around you,

the excess fabric flares

or drapes elegantly.

I also tried incorporating

artistic forms and details.

Geometric figures can produce beautiful shapes.

My aim is to rebuild patterns

using a variety of methods.

Wearing a balloon (See page 27 for instructions)

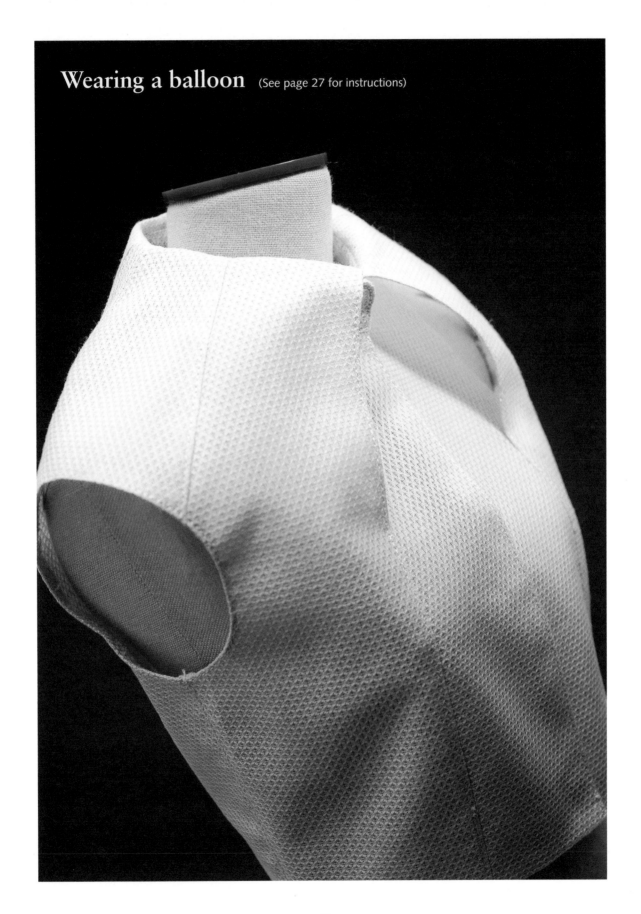

Wearing a circle (See page 28 for instructions)

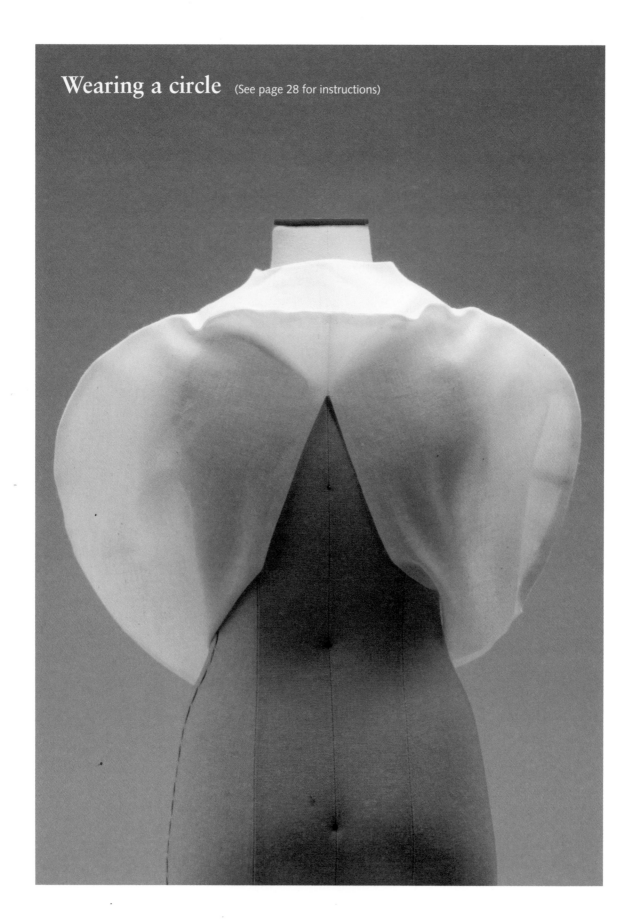

Wearing a circle (See page 30 for instructions)

Wearing a triangle (See page 32 for instructions)

Sprouting at the back (*nyokitto*) (See page 37 for instructions)

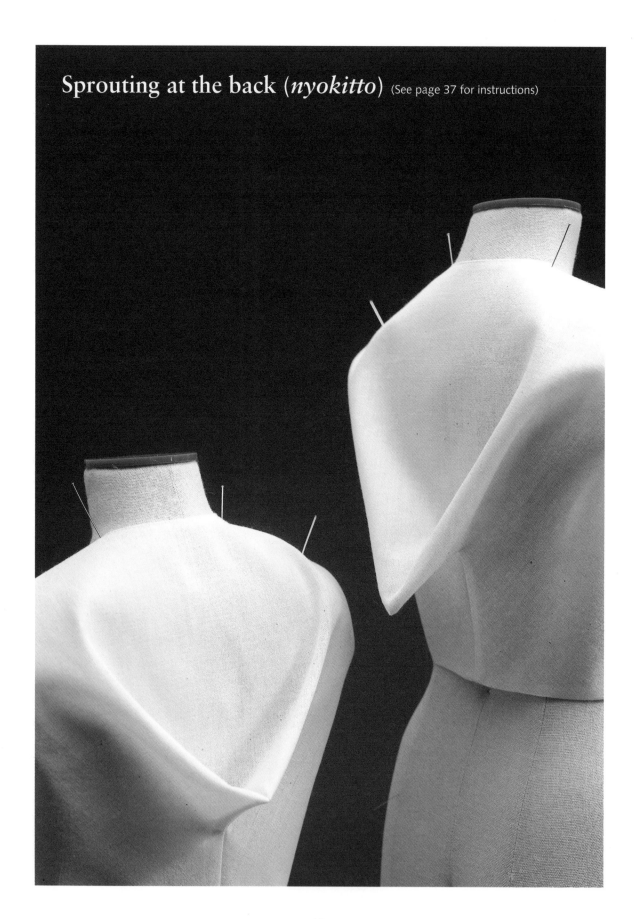

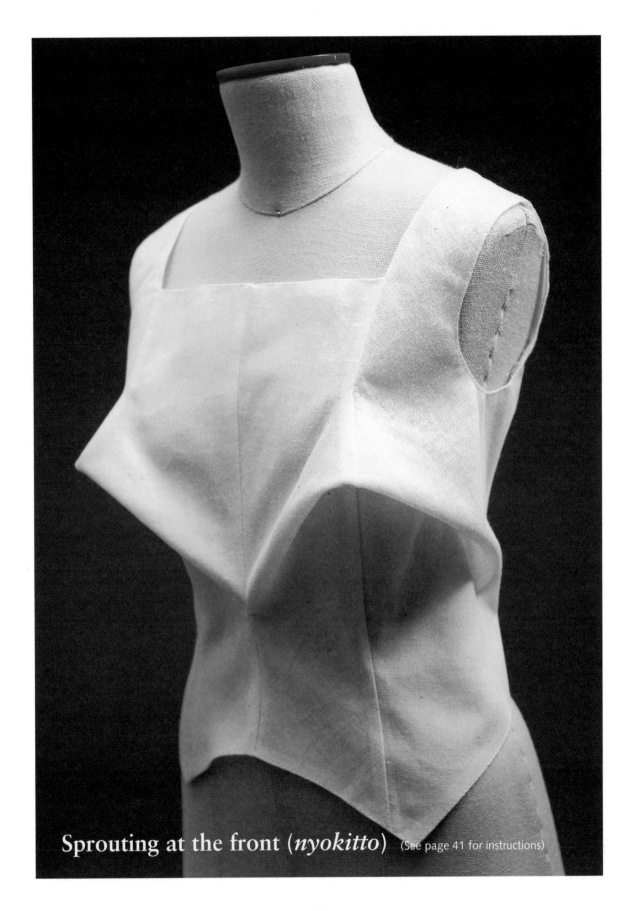

Sprouting at the front (*nyokitto*) (See page 41 for instructions)

Just like a stole (See page 42 for instructions)

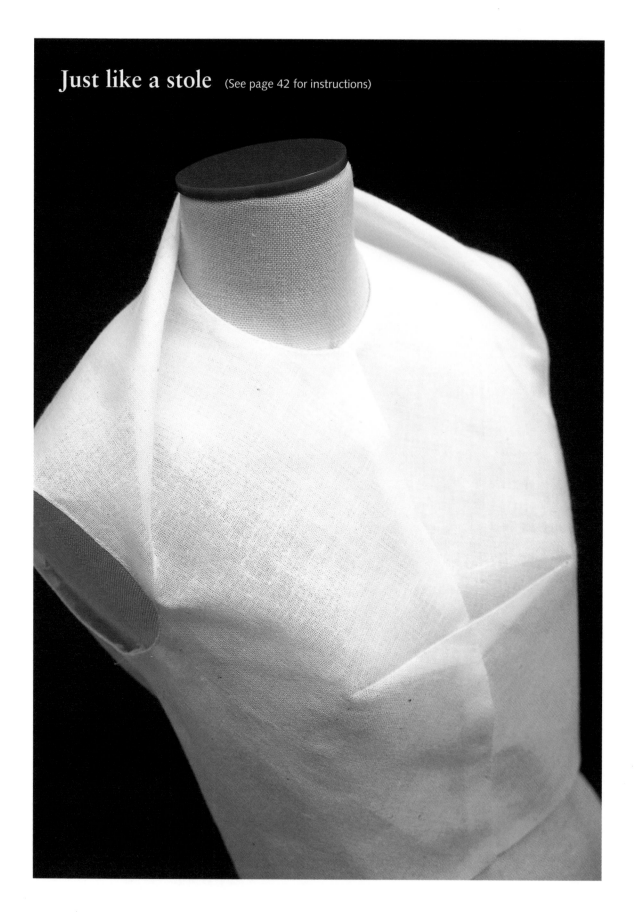

A ball-shaped accordion (*jabara*) (See page 45 for instructions)

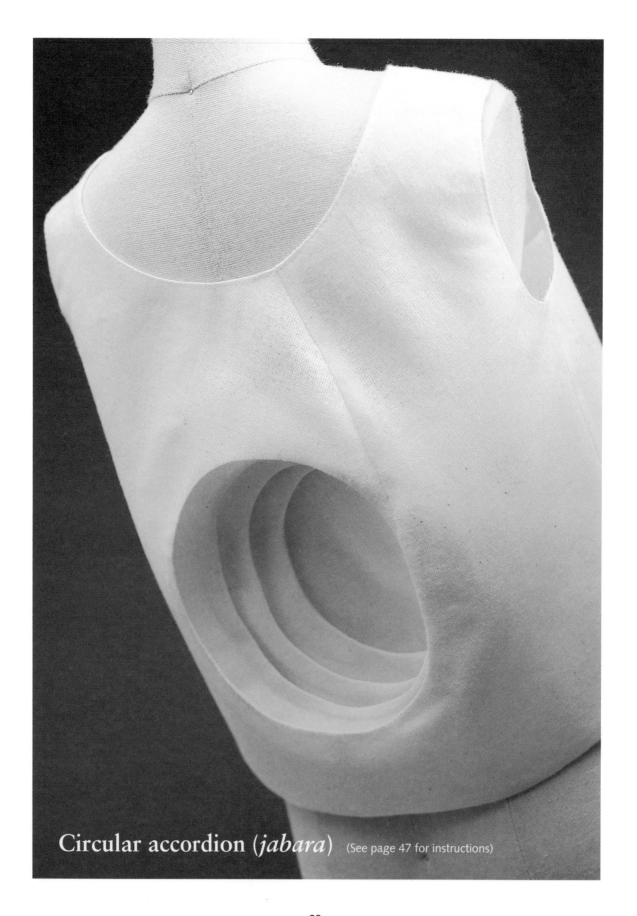

Circular accordion (*jabara*) (See page 47 for instructions)

Circular sleeve (See page 49 for instructions)

Square accordion (*jabara*)

(See page 50 for instructions)

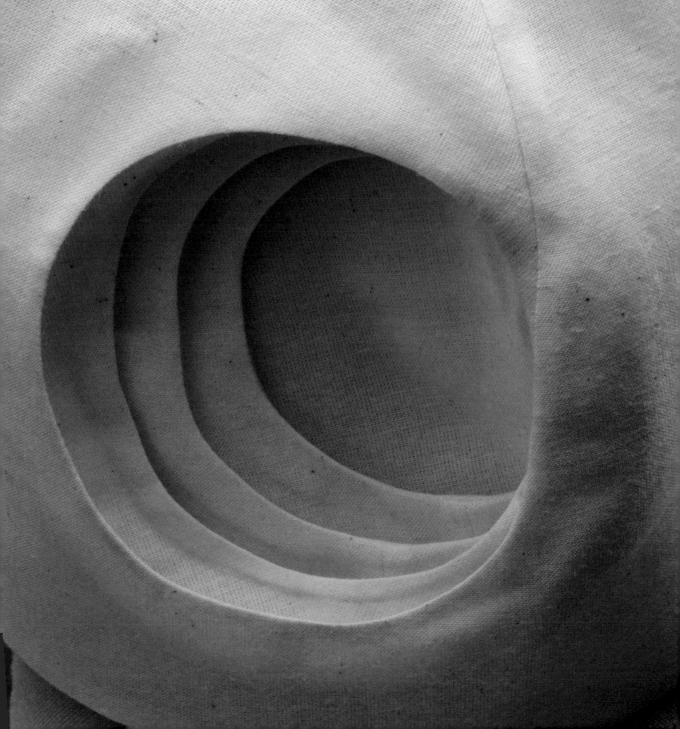

Pattern-making based on the concept of "playing with geometrics"

Wearing a balloon

I came up with this design after seeing a photograph of a balloon floating gently in the sky.
It's difficult to express a form that floats over the body using three-dimensional cutting but
by expanding the design lines I added to the sloper (block) and discovered ways to turn a beautiful balloon into
a garment.

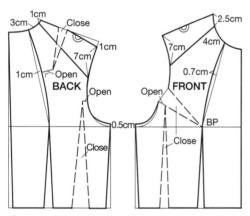

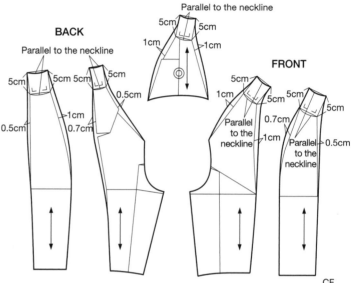

❶ Draw well-balanced design lines on the sloper (block).

❷ Close all the darts.
• Because the garment inflates from a point above the neckline, make the neckline 5cm higher than the original neckline and then copy the original neckline.
• Add 0.5–1cm each to the sides for horizontal expansion and draw a smooth, continuous line.
• Because the centre front line is curved, the extension is cut on the bias.
• Where the lengths are not the same when the design lines created by adding an amount for expansion are sewn together, correct the length by easing or stretching the fabric. Where the difference in length is particularly noticeable, adjust at the neckline.

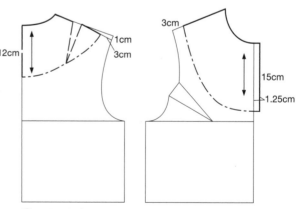

❸ Widen the facing, as the area around the shoulders tends to stand up.

Page 13: Wearing a balloon

The large collar attached to the collar band gently expands and becomes part of the bodice.

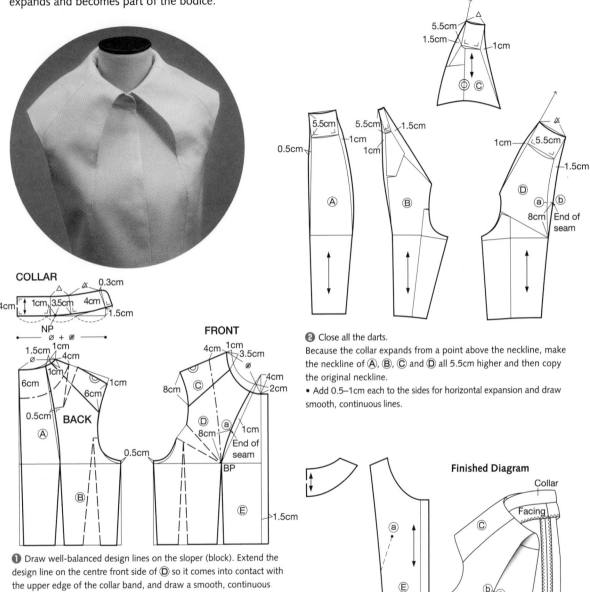

COLLAR

FRONT

BACK

❶ Draw well-balanced design lines on the sloper (block). Extend the design line on the centre front side of Ⓓ so it comes into contact with the upper edge of the collar band, and draw a smooth, continuous line passing through the BP. Draw the 4cm-wide collar band (that also serves as a facing).

❷ Close all the darts.
Because the collar expands from a point above the neckline, make the neckline of Ⓐ, Ⓑ, Ⓒ and Ⓓ all 5.5cm higher and then copy the original neckline.
• Add 0.5–1cm each to the sides for horizontal expansion and draw smooth, continuous lines.

Finished Diagram

❸ Draft the pattern for the facing. Ⓔ serves as both bodice front and facing. Finally, align ⓐ and ⓑ and sew up to the end of the seam.

Page 14: Wearing a circle

I tried joining two circular pieces of fabric
to gently enclose the body and
accentuate the curve.

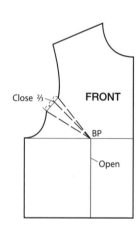

FRONT

Close ⅔

BP

Open

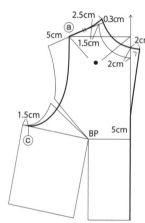

2.5cm   0.3cm

5cm   ⓐ

1.5cm   2cm

2cm

1.5cm

ⓒ   BP   5cm

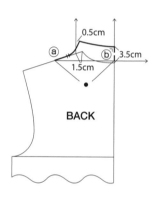

0.5cm

ⓐ   ⓑ   3.5cm

1.5cm

BACK

❶ Close ⅔ of the armhole darts on the
sloper (block).

❷ Draw a high neckline. As a shortage will
occur at the front neckline, add extra width at
the centre front. Determine the width of the
shoulders and mark it ⓐ.

❸ Do the same for the back as for the front.
Draw a high neckline and measure ⓐ, which
is the same length as the front shoulder width.
Extend the line from ⓐ, and mark as ⓑ the
point where it comes into contact with the
centre back.

Front

Back

The folded garment.

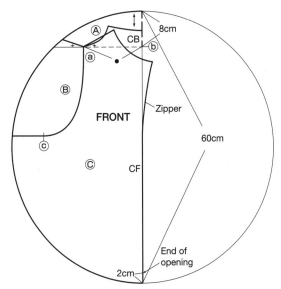

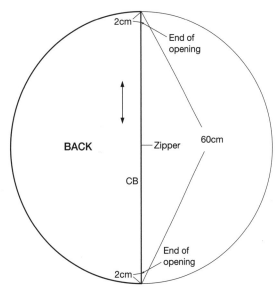

❹ Draw a circle with a radius of 30cm. Measure 8cm from the circumference on the diameter, and from there take ● measurement to mark ⓐ. Align ⓐ on the bodice front and back. Extend ⓐ–ⓒ towards the circumference of the circle. You may draw the line at any angle from ⓒ, but here I have drawn it horizontally. Draw another line passing through ⓐ, with equal angles between the horizontal line that passes through ⓐ and the front shoulder line.

❺ For the bodice back, the pattern is two aligned semicircular pieces. I made the centre back into a zipper opening.

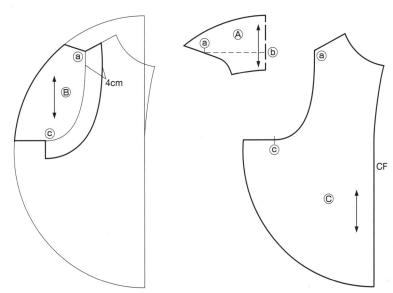

❻ The pattern for the bodice front consists of three parts.
Ⓐ: On the line between ⓐ and ⓑ, reverse as shown in the above drawing and copy.
Ⓑ: As the section that is concealed in the armhole of the bodice front is required for coverage, add 4cm of width parallel to the armhole.

Page 15: Wearing a circle

Here, the body emerges perpendicularly from the circle, making the dress appear conical in shape.

The form changes according to the position and size of the opening in the hem and the weight of the fabric.

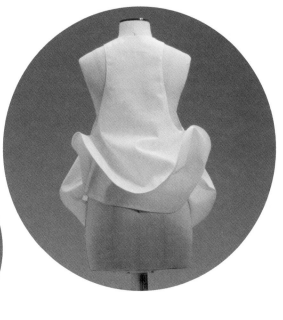

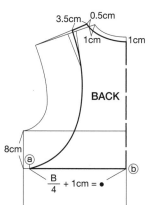

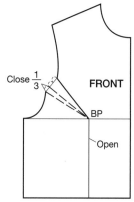

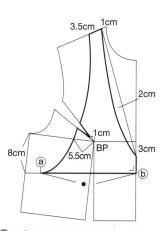

BACK

3.5cm 0.5cm

1cm 1cm

8cm

ⓐ ⓑ

$$\frac{B}{4} + 1cm = •$$

❶ Decide where the body is to emerge, measure body width and mark it ⓐ–ⓑ.

Close $\frac{1}{3}$ **FRONT**

BP

Open

❷ Close the armhole darts and cut and open out.

FRONT back diagram:

3.5cm 1cm

2cm

1cm

BP

8cm ⓐ 5.5cm 3cm

ⓑ

❸ In the same way as the bodice back, measure body width measurement on the bodice front.

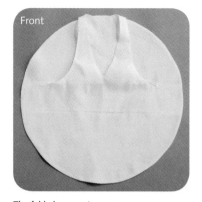

Front

Back

The folded garment.

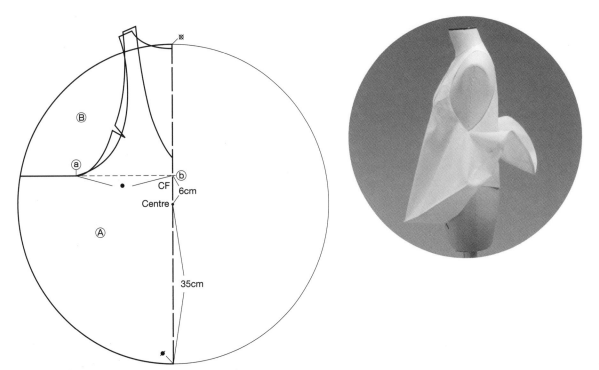

④ Draw a circle with a radius of 35cm, decide where you want the body to emerge on the centre front, and mark the position ⓑ. From ⓑ measure ● on the horizontal line and mark point ⓐ. Align ⓐ–ⓑ and copy the bodice front and back.

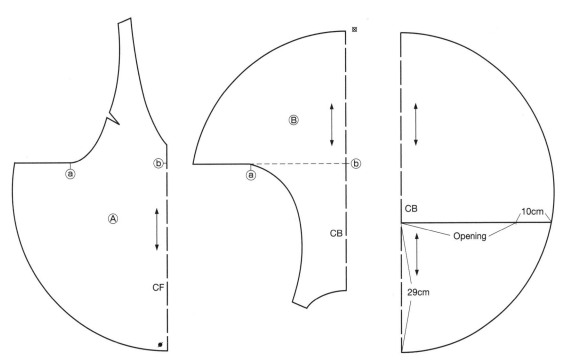

⑤ The pattern consists of bodice front Ⓐ and bodice back Ⓑ. Reverse the pattern for Ⓑ on the line ⓐ–ⓑ and copy.

⑥ Adjust the length of the opening on the underside of the garment with snaps or buttons after trying it on.

31

Page 16: Wearing a triangle

By placing triangular pieces of fabric over a dress form I created a garment that resembles an objet d'art.

I made the triangles exceptionally sharp, and several new shapes were created by placing the garment on a three-dimensional form.

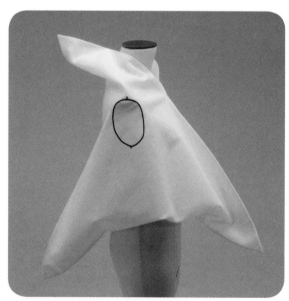

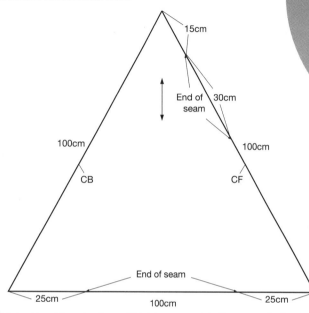

① Cut out two triangular pieces of fabric large enough to fit over your body. Here I cut out an equilateral triangle of sides 100cm and made openings for the head and the hem. A zipper opening would also be interesting. Adjust after completion.

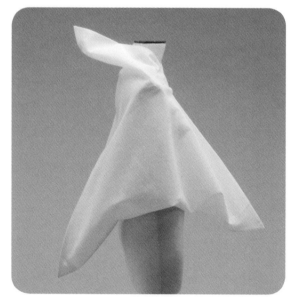

② Place the triangular pieces of fabric you have sewn together on a dress form.

③ Mark the positions of the armholes on the fabric.

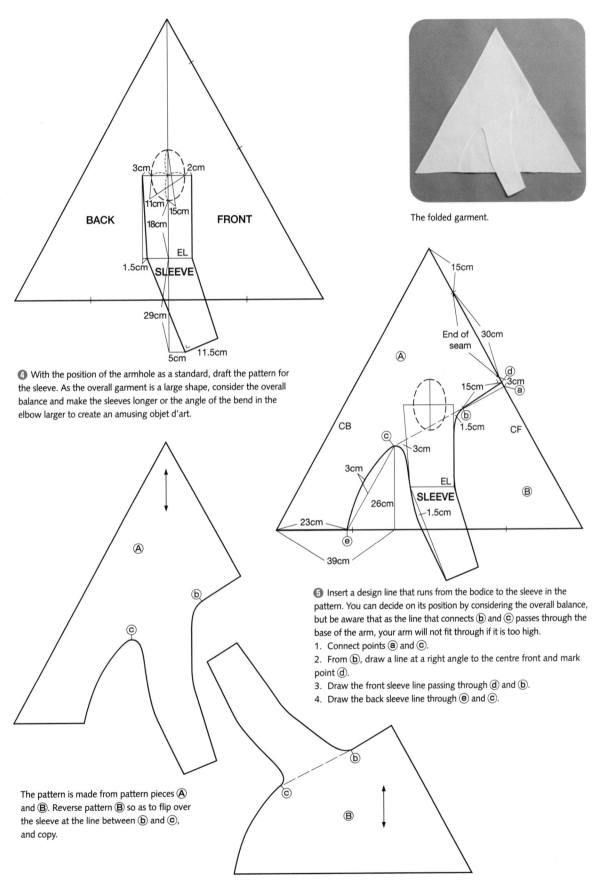

BACK

FRONT

3cm / 2cm

11cm

15cm

18cm

EL

1.5cm **SLEEVE**

29cm

5cm   11.5cm

The folded garment.

❹ With the position of the armhole as a standard, draft the pattern for the sleeve. As the overall garment is a large shape, consider the overall balance and make the sleeves longer or the angle of the bend in the elbow larger to create an amusing objet d'art.

15cm

Ⓐ

End of
seam   30cm

ⓓ
3cm
ⓐ

15cm

ⓑ

1.5cm

CB

ⓒ   3cm

CF

3cm

EL

26cm   **SLEEVE**

Ⓑ

1.5cm

23cm

ⓔ

39cm

❺ Insert a design line that runs from the bodice to the sleeve in the pattern. You can decide on its position by considering the overall balance, but be aware that as the line that connects ⓑ and ⓒ passes through the base of the arm, your arm will not fit through if it is too high.
1. Connect points ⓐ and ⓒ.
2. From ⓑ, draw a line at a right angle to the centre front and mark point ⓓ.
3. Draw the front sleeve line passing through ⓓ and ⓑ.
4. Draw the back sleeve line through ⓔ and ⓒ.

Ⓐ

ⓑ

ⓒ

ⓑ

ⓒ

Ⓑ

The pattern is made from pattern pieces Ⓐ and Ⓑ. Reverse pattern Ⓑ so as to flip over the sleeve at the line between ⓑ and ⓒ, and copy.

A pullover that uses most of a square piece of fabric and requires a minimum of measurement and sewing.
A garment made with simple straight seams.
It would be interesting to make up this simple garment in a stretch fabric.

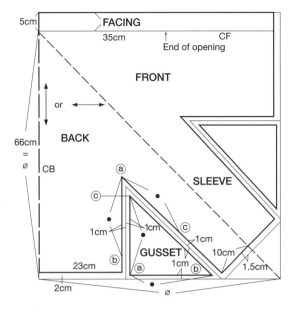

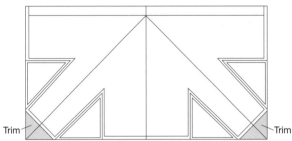

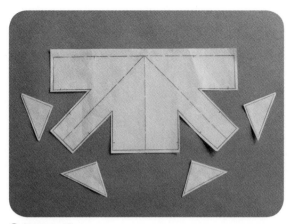

1 Cutting guide.

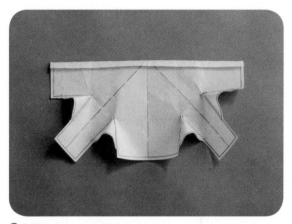

2 Fold the facing and attach the gore.

Drafting a pattern with your own measurements

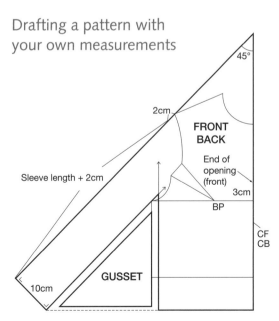

From the centre front line, draw the shoulder measured at an angle of 45 degrees and the sleeve cap line. Place the front bodice sloper (block) here, and decide the ease in the bodice width, garment length and sleeve length, etc.

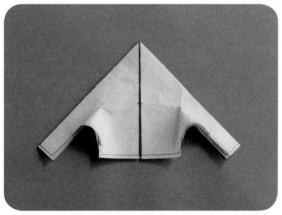

3 Sew from the centre front hem to the end of the opening. Sew the underarm, the gore and the sides, and fold up the sleeve openings and the hem. Attach zipper to the length of the centre front and design the opening in any way you want.

Sprouting at the back (*nyokitto*)

In this garment, a fold in the fabric protrudes from a fitted bodice.

The size of the protrusion can be changed by making the angle larger or smaller.

This intriguing design is more contemporary than a draped design but is equally elegant.

Make a *nyokitto* design from a flat piece of fabric

A

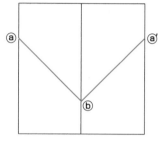

❶ Decide where you want to place the protrusion (ⓐ–ⓑ–ⓐ').

❷ Because the bodice left and right are symmetrical, make only one side of the pattern. Open out twice the desired height of the protrusion (ⓑ–ⓒ) with ⓐ as the pivotal point. Mark ⓑ' and connect ⓑ and ⓑ' with a straight line. ⓐ–ⓒ–ⓑ is a right angle.

As shown in the photograph, to cause ⓒ to protrude at an acute angle, determine the position of ⓒ on the mountain fold line that has been extended beyond the line connecting ⓑ–ⓑ'.

B

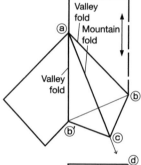

C

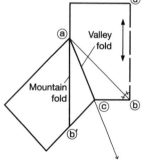

To make the protrusion flat as shown in photograph C, bring ⓒ closer to ⓐ until the angle at ⓑ is a right angle. Various expressions can be created by moving the position of ⓒ.

D

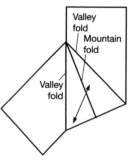

The fold protrudes at 90 degrees as shown in photograph A, but if you use the bias on the mountain fold, the result is a curved soft look.

Page 18: *Nyokitto* at the back

I introduced a *nyokitto* on this bodice back. Protruding from the back of a fitted bodice, it looks like the beak of a bird.

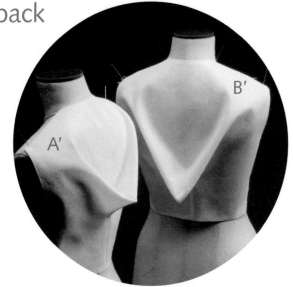

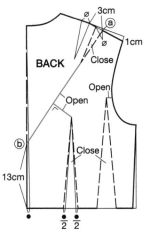

❶ Decide where you want to position the *nyokitto* (ⓐ–ⓑ). Move the shoulder darts to the ⓐ–ⓑ line.

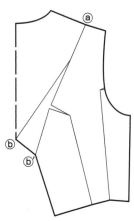

❷ Close the shoulder darts, cut and open out and mark it ⓑ'.

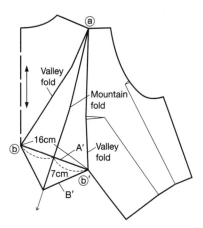

❸ Because the height will be insufficient, open out again with ⓐ as the pivotal point. Closing the waist darts will make ⓐ –ⓑ' longer than ⓐ–ⓑ, but as it is only a small amount, make it into ease along the outside edge. Depending on the method for determining the mountain fold line, either the *nyokitto* A' or B' shown above will form.

Nyokitto at the front (See page 40 for instructions)

This *nyokitto* rises from the bodice front.
The softly draped fabric, cut on the bias, adds impact to the subtle shape.
Choose any angle you want—it's up to you. Try combining angles for a more interesting look.

Page 38: *Nyokitto* at the front

A *nyokitto* that protrudes at a right angle from the bodice front.

The fabric is cut on the bias.

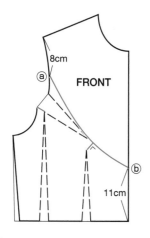

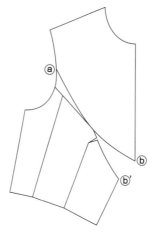

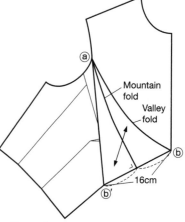

❶ Decide where you want to position the *nyokitto* (ⓐ–ⓑ).

❷ The ⓑ–ⓑ' measurement is insufficient even after closing all the darts.

❸ With ⓐ as the pivotal point, further cut and open out the shortage (in this case, 16cm). Use the bias on the mountain fold.

Page 39: *Nyokitto* at the front

The *nyokitto* runs from the shoulder and frames the decolletage like a necklace.

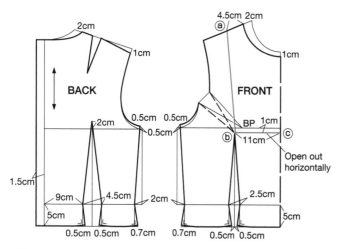

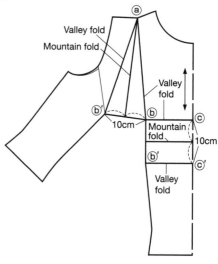

❶ A blouse that has been slightly lengthened from the waistline. Insert cutting and opening out lines ⓐ–ⓑ–ⓒ on the bodice front. Move the armhole darts to ⓑ.

❷ Close the armhole darts. Open out ⓑ–ⓒ in a parallel line (in this case, 10cm) and mark the new line ⓑ'–ⓒ'. Open ⓐ–ⓑ as well (in this case, 10cm) and mark the new line ⓐ–ⓑ'.

Page 19: *Nyokitto* at the front

A folded *nyokitto* that creates
the effect of a double-layered blouse.

You can make the fabric protrude
in any way you want according to
the position of the design lines
and the length of the mountain folds.

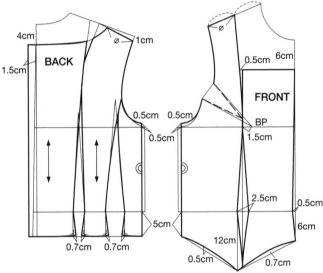

1 Draft the base pattern for the blouse.

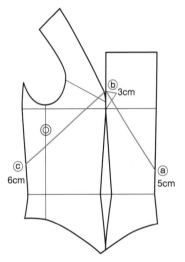

2 Align the side seams of the bodice front and back and close the armhole darts. Draw ⓐ–ⓑ–ⓒ where you want to position the *nyokitto*.

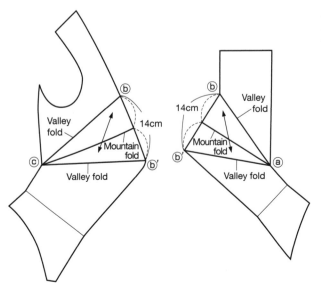

3 With both ⓐ and ⓒ as pivotal points, cut and open out (in this case, 14cm). Use the bias on the mountain fold.

Page 20: Just like a stole

A look where you appear to be wearing a stole is created with one piece of fabric that protrudes from the bodice along the shoulder.

Change the look of the stole by the way you draw the cutting and opening out lines.

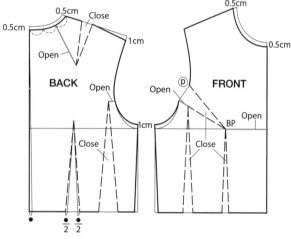

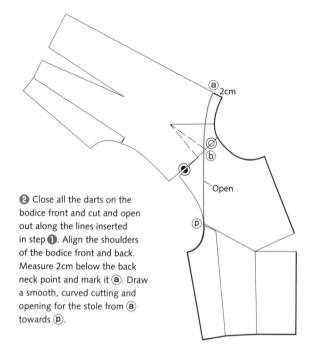

❶ Draft the pattern. As the neckline is too high, trim it on the sloper. On the bodice front, draw cutting and opening out lines toward the centre front horizontally from the bust point.

❷ Close all the darts on the bodice front and cut and open out along the lines inserted in step ❶. Align the shoulders of the bodice front and back. Measure 2cm below the back neck point and mark it ⓐ. Draw a smooth, curved cutting and opening for the stole from ⓐ towards ⓟ.

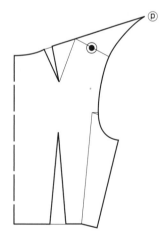

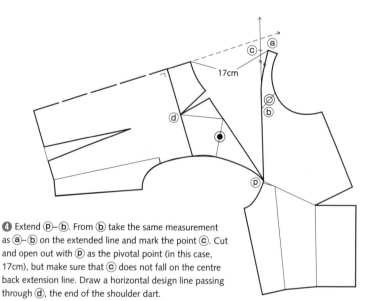

❸ Move the shoulder darts to the neckline. Align what is left of the front and back shoulders.

❹ Extend ⓟ–ⓑ. From ⓑ take the same measurement as ⓐ–ⓑ on the extended line and mark the point ⓒ. Cut and open out with ⓟ as the pivotal point (in this case, 17cm), but make sure that ⓒ does not fall on the centre back extension line. Draw a horizontal design line passing through ⓓ, the end of the shoulder dart.

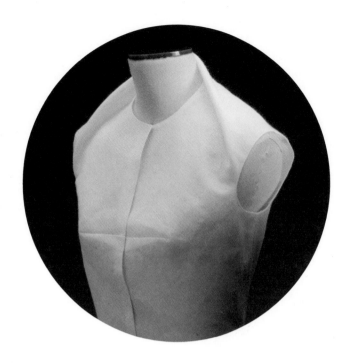

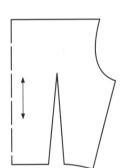

5 A pattern for the bottom point of the bodice back.

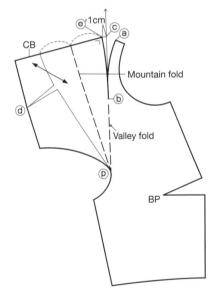

CB

e 1cm c a

Mountain fold

d

Valley fold

p

BP

6 Close the shoulder darts with ⓓ as the pivotal point until the extension line of the centre back crosses ⓒ. Measure 1cm on the extension line from ⓒ and mark it ⓔ. Sew along ⓔ–ⓑ–ⓐ to form a dart.

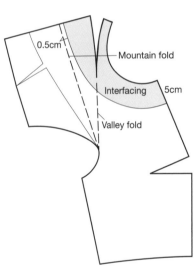

0.5cm

Mountain fold

Interfacing 5cm

Valley fold

7 If the neckline does not settle when the garment is worn, either use interfacing or edge-stitch halfway along the valley fold as a means of preventing stretching of the neckline.

A ball-shaped accordion (*jabara*)

I'll never forget the fun of playing with paper
when I was a child, folding it
to create different forms.

You can create a ball by folding
several sheets of paper in alternating
crescent-moon shapes.

The sharp accents created
by the semicircular accordion shape
create delicate sleeve detail.

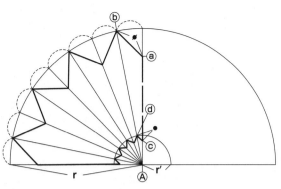

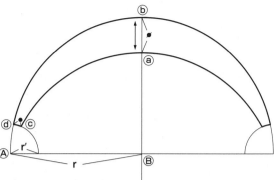

❶ With Ⓐ as the pivotal point, draw a semicircle of radius r.

❷ With Ⓐ as the pivotal point, draw another semicircle of radius r'.

❸ Divide the perimeter of both semicircles into the number of folds you are going to make in the sleeve.

❹ Determine the width of each fold on both semicircles, then draw them in jagged lines to complete the cross-sectional diagram.
ⓐ–ⓑ = ✒   ⓒ–ⓓ = •

❺ With Ⓑ as the pivotal point, draw a semicircle of radius r.

❻ With Ⓐ as the pivotal point, draw a semicircle of radius r'.

❼ Draw a line directly upwards from Ⓑ, and make the point where it meets the perimeter of the outermost semicircle ⓑ.

❽ From ⓑ, measure the predetermined fold width ✒ and mark it ⓐ.

❾ Make the point where the r and r' semicircles intersect ⓓ.

❿ From ⓓ measure the fold width of the inner semicircle • on the perimeter of the semicircle r, and mark it ⓒ.

⓫ Find the centre of the circle, the circumference of which passes through ⓒ and ⓐ, on the line directly downward from Ⓑ and mark it Ⓧ.

⓬ With Ⓧ as the pivotal point, draw an arc to make the crescent-moon shape. This crescent-moon shape becomes the pattern for the *jabara*. As many pattern pieces as the number of folds are necessary.

When opened out	When folded	When pulled diagonally

Page 21: A ball-shaped *jabara*

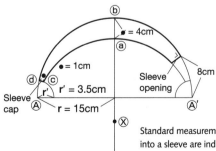

Standard measurements for making this pattern into a sleeve are indicated here. Measure 8cm above Ⓐ', and draw a line at a right angle from that point to make the sleeve opening. The sleeve is constructed with 16 pattern pieces of the crescent-moon shape. Position the sleeve so that it sits well on the arm.

45

circular *jabara*

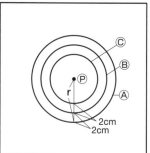

❶ With Ⓟ as the pivotal point, make a circle Ⓐ of radius r.
With Ⓟ as the pivotal point, make circle Ⓑ of radius r – 2cm.
With Ⓟ as the pivotal point, make circle Ⓒ of radius r – 4cm.

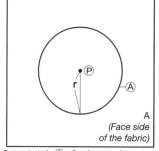

❷ Cut out circle Ⓐ of radius r on base A.

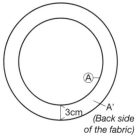

❸ Draw another circle around circle Ⓐ at a distance of 3cm. Mark as A', the doughnut-shaped portion between the two circles. A' becomes the underside of A.

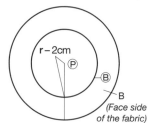

❹ Mark as B the doughnut-shaped portion between circle Ⓑ and the outer circumference of A'.

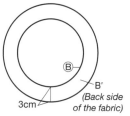

❺ Draw another circle around circle Ⓑ at a distance of 3cm. Mark as B' the doughnut-shaped portion between the two circles. B' becomes the underside of Ⓑ.

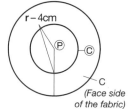

❻ Mark as C the doughnut-shaped portion between circle Ⓒ and the outer circumference of B'.

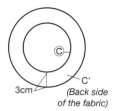

❼ Draw another circle around circle Ⓒ at a distance of 3cm. Mark as C' the doughnut-shaped portion between the two circles. C' becomes the underside of C.

⬤ A and A' are sewn together and A' and B are sewn together along the outer circumference.
In a similar manner, B and B' and C and C' are attached to construct the *jabara*.

Page 22: Circular *jabara*

The circles in the vicinity of the back waist gradually become smaller as they move towards the inside and eventually seem to disappear into a tunnel. The effect is subtle and mysterious.

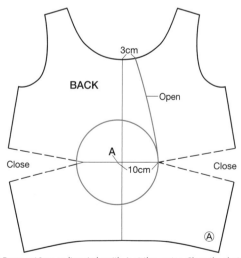

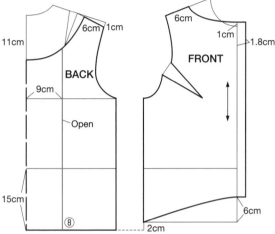

❶ Draft a pattern for the bodice base. To make the bodice back separate from the body, add ease by cutting and opening out. The *jabara* design makes the bodice back heavy. To counter this, raise the neckline at the centre front.

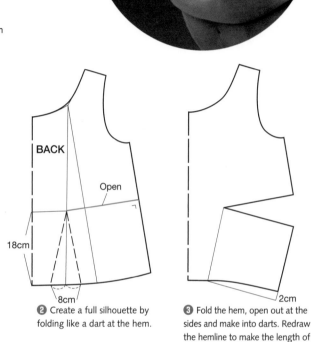

❷ Create a full silhouette by folding like a dart at the hem.

❸ Fold the hem, open out at the sides and make into darts. Redraw the hemline to make the length of the bodice back the same as that of the bodice front side seam.

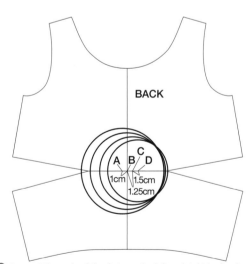

❹ Connect the ends of the darts on the left and right bodice back panels, and draw circles with A, B, C and D as their respective centres. By moving the centres to the right each circle is moved to the right. Draw a 10cm-radius circle with A at the centre; a 9cm-radius circle with B at the centre; an 8cm-radius circle with C at the centre; and a 7cm-radius circle with D at the centre.
As each of these circles pass through the bust darts, the *jabara* takes on a three-dimensional structure.

❺ Draw a 10cm-radius circle with A at the centre. Close the darts and cut and open out at the neckline.

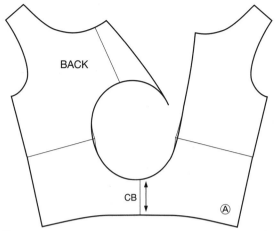

BACK

CB

Ⓐ

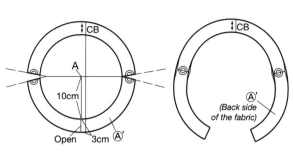

↕ CB

A

10cm

Open   3cm Ⓐ'

↕ CB

Ⓐ'
(Back side of the fabric)

6 Redraw the circumference of the circle. Mark the bodice back as Ⓐ.

7 Create the *jabara* like a facing on the underside of Ⓐ. With A as the centre, draw a 13cm-radius circle (3cm added as the depth of the *jabara*), and mark it Ⓐ'. Align the darts on Ⓐ', cut and open out at the bottom of the circle and make it the seam. Redraw the circle to form a smooth curve. Ⓐ' becomes the underside of A.

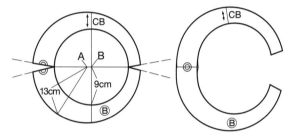

↕ CB   ↕ CB

A B

9cm

13cm

Ⓑ

Ⓑ

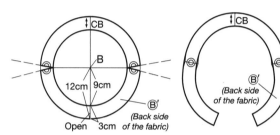

↕ CB   ↕ CB

B

12cm 9cm

Open 3cm   *(Back side of the fabric)*

Ⓑ'

Ⓑ'
(Back side of the fabric)

8 Draw a 9cm-radius circle with B at the centre. To connect it to Ⓐ' on the underside, with A at the centre draw a circle that has the same circumference (13cm-radius circle) as the outer edge of Ⓐ'. To make sure the seams are not noticeable, place the joint in the sides. Align the darts and correct the lines.

9 Draw a 12cm-radius circle with B at the centre. Of that 3cm is the depth of the *jabara*. Make the pattern for Ⓑ' in the same way as for Ⓐ'.

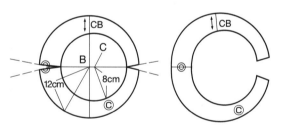

↕ CB   ↕ CB

B   C

12cm 8cm

Ⓒ

Ⓒ

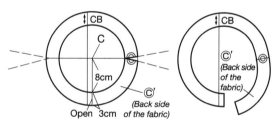

↕ CB   ↕ CB

C

8cm

Ⓒ'
(Back side of the fabric)

Open 3cm
(Back side of the fabric)

Ⓒ'
(Back side of the fabric)

10 Make the pattern for Ⓒ in the same way as in **8**.

11 Make the pattern for Ⓒ' in the same way as in **9**.

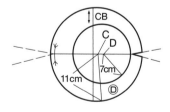

↕ CB

C D

7cm

11cm

Ⓓ

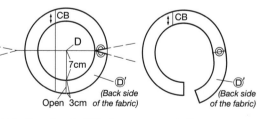

↕ CB   ↕ CB

D

7cm

Open 3cm   *(Back side of the fabric)*

Ⓓ'
(Back side of the fabric)

Ⓓ'
(Back side of the fabric)

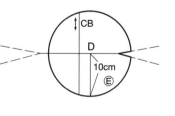

↕ CB

D

10cm

Ⓔ

12 Make the pattern for Ⓓ in the same way as in **10**.

13 Make the pattern for Ⓓ' in the same way as in **11**.

14 Draw a circle that has the same circumference as the outer edge of Ⓓ' and call it Ⓔ.

● To sew, turn Ⓐ and Ⓐ', Ⓑ and Ⓑ', Ⓒ and Ⓒ', and Ⓓ and Ⓓ' inside out, sew the circles on the inside and turn back to the right side. Next sew the outer edges of Ⓐ' and Ⓑ, Ⓑ' and Ⓒ, Ⓒ' and Ⓓ, and Ⓓ' and Ⓔ.

Page 23: Circular sleeve

When placed horizontally the three-dimensional sleeve, created from one large, one medium and one small circle, will become a flat *jabara* resembling a cap sleeve.

Connect several of these circles together to make what looks like the arms of a robot.

Use a fabric that can withstand a permanent finish.

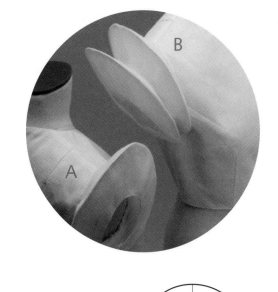

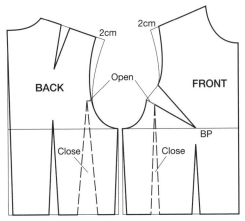

❶ Draft a pattern for the bodice. Because the design has a broad-shouldered look, make the armhole 2cm deeper.

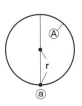

❷ Calculate the radius using the formula below (2cm has been added to the armhole for seam allowance), and draw circle Ⓐ. This becomes the sleeve-attachment line.

r = (AH + 2)/6.28

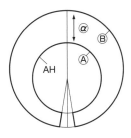

❸ Draw circle Ⓑ, which will form the outer edge of the sleeve. Make it any size you want, but here r′= 12cm. Mark 2.5cm from point ⓐ on the underarm to get the r′ measurement.

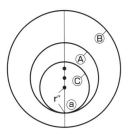

❹ Draw the circle Ⓒ for the sleeve opening. Calculate the radius r″ for circle Ⓒ.

r″= (sleeve opening measurement + 2cm (room) + 2cm (seam allowance))/6.28

The sleeve opening measurement is measured as a circle at a point 5–6cm below the sleeve-attachment line on the shoulder line.

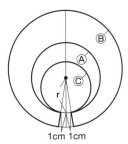

❺ Measure 1cm as seam allowance on either side of r and connect to the circle centre.

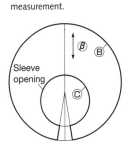

❻ Mark the pattern comprising circles Ⓐ and Ⓑ as ⓐ, and the pattern comprising circles Ⓑ and Ⓒ as β̂.
The sleeve is made up of these two patterns.

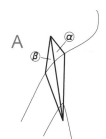

The circular sleeve is made by attaching the two patterns. The pattern is the same as A, but the ⓐ pattern is made from three pieces and the β̂ pattern is made from one. As you increase the number of pieces, you have to consider the width of the sleeve opening and the position of the sleeve-opening circle.

Page 24: Square *jabara*

Layered squares give this *jabara*
a sharp, well-defined look.

The way they become increasingly and regularly smaller,
as if they have been graded, shows off the beauty
of the garment even further.

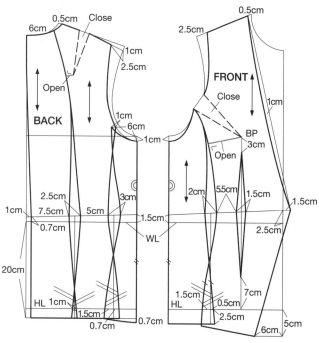

❶ Draft a pattern for the vest using a design that is fitted at the waist
and with a flare in the hem.

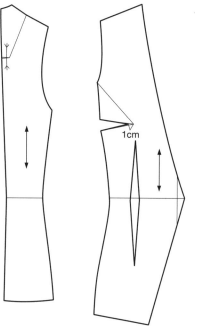

❷ Fold the shoulder darts and chest darts and develop the pattern.

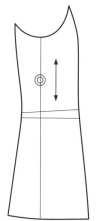

❸ Make the *jabara* on the left
bodice panel.

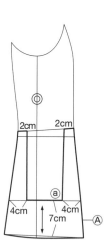

❹ The side piece on the bottommost
layer of the *jabara* will be the section
below the high waist. Make a U-
shaped opening in the centre and
mark it Ⓐ.

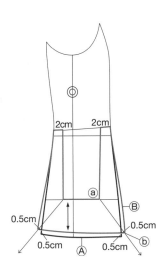

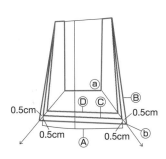

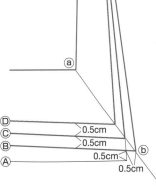

5 Make Ⓑ, the second *jabara* that connects to Ⓐ, 0.5cm shorter and 0.5cm wider than Ⓐ, and mark the corner that is created ⓑ. Connect ⓐ and ⓑ with a straight line. Do the same on the other side too. Make *jabara* Ⓒ 0.5cm shorter than Ⓑ, and create a corner on the line ⓐ–ⓑ. Then make *jabara* Ⓓ 0.5cm shorter than Ⓒ.

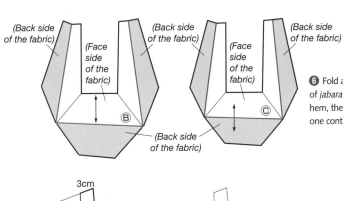

6 Fold and cut the side seams of *jabara* Ⓑ, Ⓒ and Ⓓ along the hem, then cut and attach to make one continuous piece.

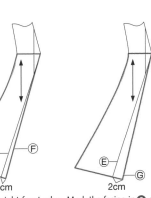

7 The pattern for the uppermost *jabara* Ⓓ is one continuous piece with the part above the waist of the bodice. Do not open holes as in Ⓐ, Ⓑ and Ⓒ.

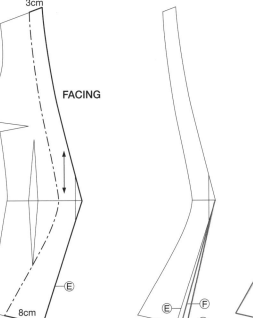

8 Draft a pattern for the facing.

9 Make the pattern for the jabara on the right front edge. Mark the facing in **8** as Ⓔ. In the same way as the jabara on the left side, make the patterns for Ⓔ and Ⓕ so that they become smaller the higher they get. As Ⓔ and Ⓕ are to be sewn and then turned inside out, two pattern pieces are required.

PATTERN MAGIC

Part 2
Decorative structures

Twisting, catching, draping—

various methods with which

to capture different qualities of the fabric

and incorporate them into elegant garments.

Create the structure of the decorative

elements on the sloper (block) base first,

and then copy them onto the fabric.

This will allow you to change the design

in any way you want.

Knots (See page 64 for instructions)

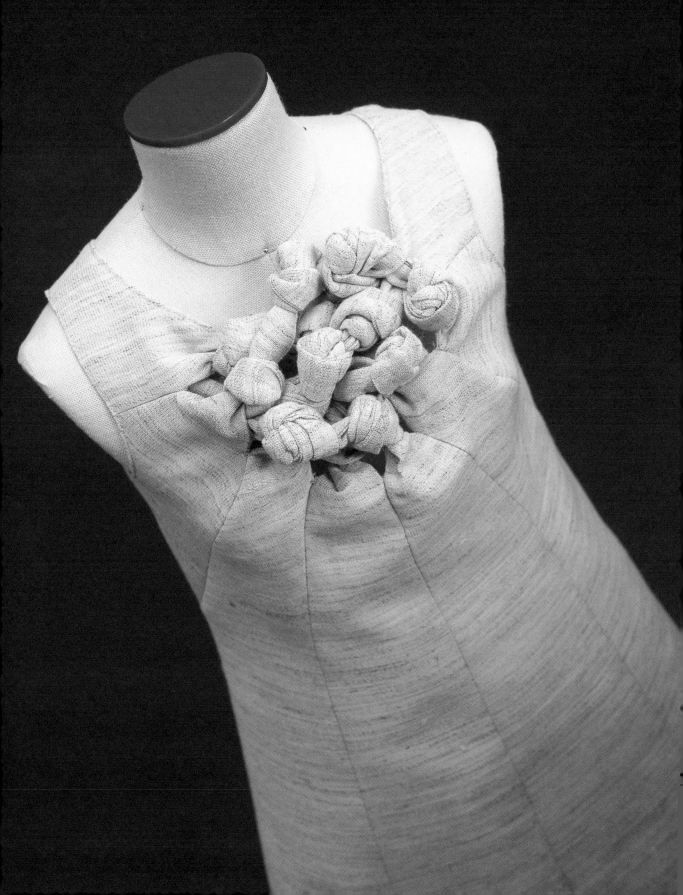

Like a jungle (See page 68 for instructions)

Stars (See page 70 for instructions)

Flip turn (See page 74 for instructions)

Different facings, different looks (See page 79 for instructions)

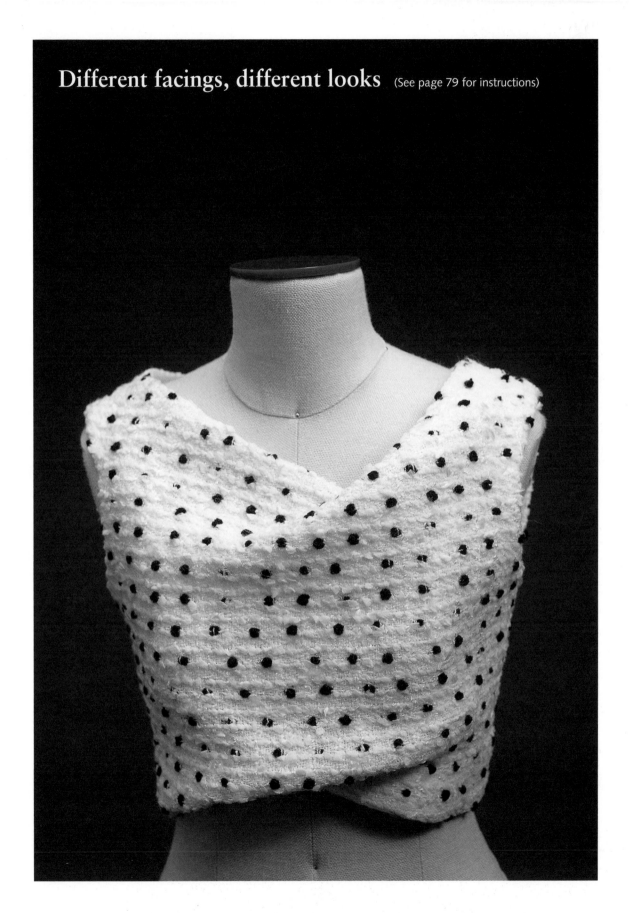

Cowl neck (See page 80 for instructions)

Application of the cowl-neck design (See page 82 for instructions)

Application of the cowl-neck design (See page 83 for instructions)

PATTERN MAGIC

Making patterns for
decorative structures

Knots

The shape created from the act of "tying" is a beautiful method of decorating garments. In this way a knotted pattern becomes a natural part of the garment.

Inserting a knot into the bodice

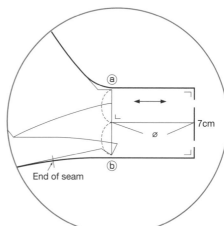

❶ Prepare a strip of fabric (7cm in width) that has been sewn along the sides and turned inside out. Measure the length of the fabric strip.

❷ Make a knot in the strip of fabric and measure the length. ∅ = length of the knot.

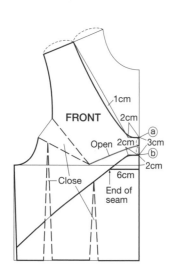

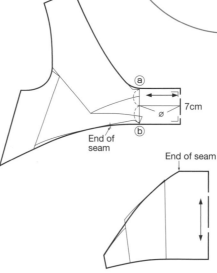

❸ Draft a pattern for the bodice front. Mark the positions of the knots ⓐ and ⓑ on the centre front. Measure 2cm from ⓐ and draw the neckline and the design lines.

❹ Close all the darts. From the position where ⓐ–ⓑ has been divided into two equal sections, measure the length of the knot ∅ and the 7cm width of the fabric strip. Redraw the lines to make smooth, continuous lines.

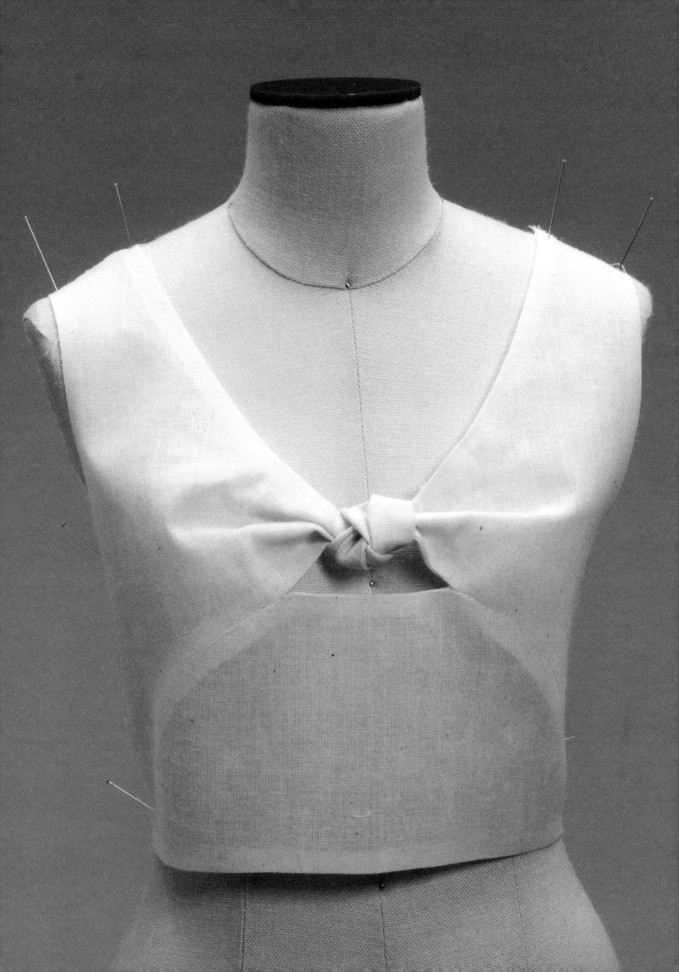

Page 53: Knots

A knotted design for a bodice.

By bringing together several knots that resemble tiny bells I have created a unique garment that evokes the sound of bells ringing.

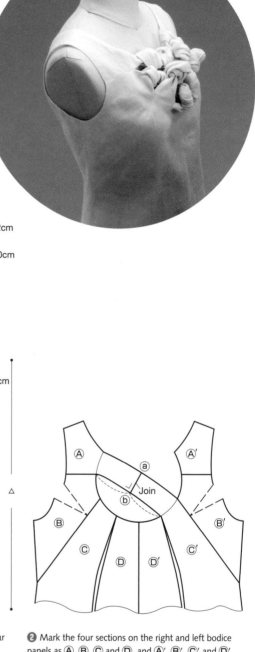

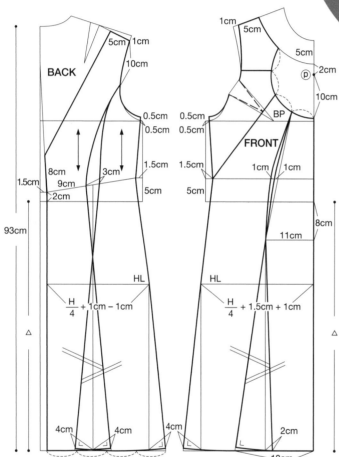

BACK

5cm 1cm
10cm

0.5cm
0.5cm

8cm 3cm
9cm
2cm 1.5cm
5cm

1.5cm

93cm

HL

$$\frac{H}{4} + 1cm - 1cm$$

4cm 4cm

1cm
5cm

5cm
2cm (p)
10cm

0.5cm BP
0.5cm

FRONT

1.5cm 1cm 1cm
5cm

8cm
11cm

HL

$$\frac{H}{4} + 1.5cm + 1cm$$

4cm 2cm
18cm

Ⓐ ⓐ Ⓐ'
    Join
Ⓑ ⓑ Ⓑ'
Ⓒ Ⓒ'
    Ⓓ Ⓓ'

❶ Draft the pattern for the bodice. With ⓟ at the centre, draw the semicircular neckline with a radius of 10cm. Divide the neckline into four equal parts, and then divide the bodice into four corresponding sections.

❷ Mark the four sections on the right and left bodice panels as Ⓐ, Ⓑ, Ⓒ and Ⓓ, and Ⓐ', Ⓑ', Ⓒ' and Ⓓ' respectively. There are various ways of making the knots in the chest area, but, to stabilize the bodice, first attach strips of knotted fabric diagonally from the left and right. Then create knots wherever you want them to be placed and fasten them in place. Firstly connect panels Ⓐ and Ⓒ' with a strip of fabric. Insert a joint along ⓐ–ⓑ halfway down the strip of fabric. To make the design symmetrical, connect Ⓐ' and Ⓒ also in the same way.

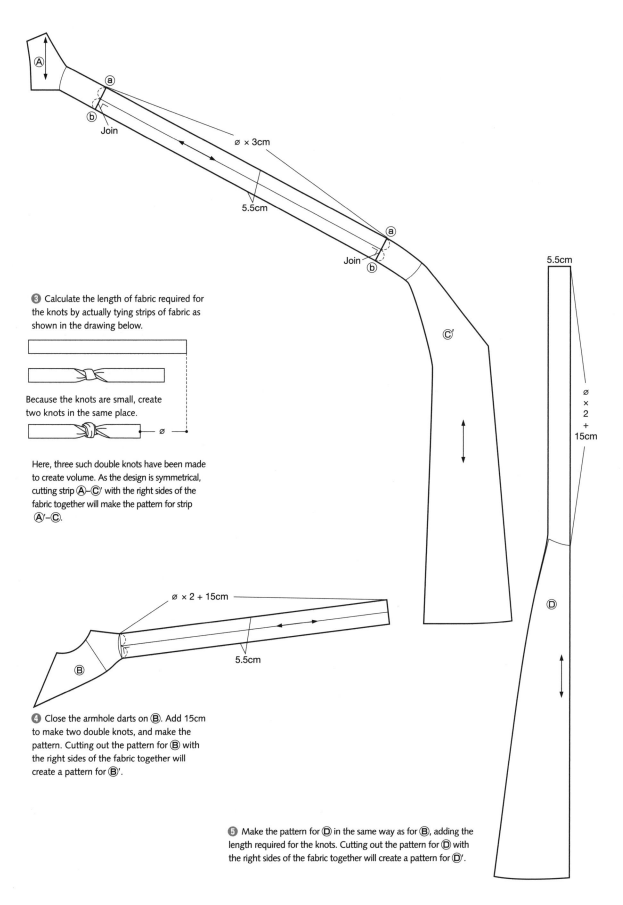

Ⓐ

ⓐ

ⓑ
Join

ø × 3cm

5.5cm

ⓐ

Join ⓑ

Ⓒ′

5.5cm

ø
×
2
+
15cm

❸ Calculate the length of fabric required for the knots by actually tying strips of fabric as shown in the drawing below.

Because the knots are small, create two knots in the same place.

ø

Here, three such double knots have been made to create volume. As the design is symmetrical, cutting strip Ⓐ–Ⓒ′ with the right sides of the fabric together will make the pattern for strip Ⓐ′–Ⓒ.

ø × 2 + 15cm

5.5cm

Ⓑ

Ⓓ

❹ Close the armhole darts on Ⓑ. Add 15cm to make two double knots, and make the pattern. Cutting out the pattern for Ⓑ with the right sides of the fabric together will create a pattern for Ⓑ′.

❺ Make the pattern for Ⓓ in the same way as for Ⓑ, adding the length required for the knots. Cutting out the pattern for Ⓓ with the right sides of the fabric together will create a pattern for Ⓓ′.

After attaching the diagonal strips, place the garment on a dress form, and closely knot the other four strips. Fasten the knots by sewing at points that cannot be seen from the outside.

Page 54: Like a jungle

A design where lines criss-cross and overlap freely on the bodice in a way that is almost organic.

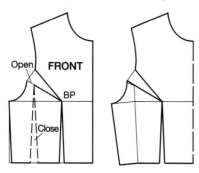

❶ Cut off the dart allowances on the sloper (block).

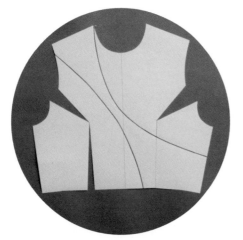

❷ Draw the first part. Draw lines in any way you want as if you were drawing a picture. When a line crosses a dart, close the particular dart and then draw the line.

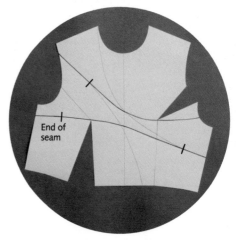

❸ Draw the second part. Mark the end of the seam.

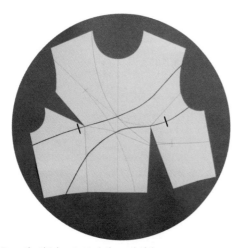

❹ Draw the third part. Mark the end of the seam.

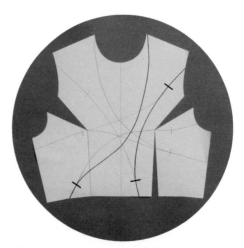

❺ Draw the fourth part. Mark the end of the seam.

Trying out different combinations of the pattern pieces is fun. Sew the right bodice only and then move the strips around to find your preferred balance for the left. When drawing the pattern parts, a variety of combinations are made possible by shortening the distance between the seam ends or making the gaps larger.

Page 55: Stars

A design that is twisted in the chest area, fitting the garment to the body in the same way as a stretch fabric. The overlapping of the fabric in a radial pattern in the front bodice creates a star shape.

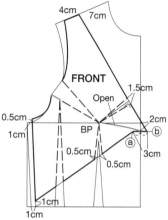

❶ Draft the pattern. As there will be excess in the neckline and the underbust when fitted exactly to the body, move the excess to the bust darts.

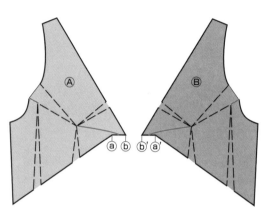

❷ Mark panels Ⓐ and Ⓑ on the left and right patterns respectively. On panel Ⓑ, mark as ⓐ' and ⓑ' the points corresponding to ⓐ and ⓑ on panel Ⓐ.

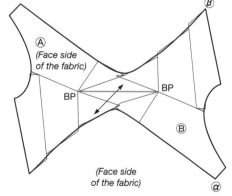

❸ Close all the darts.

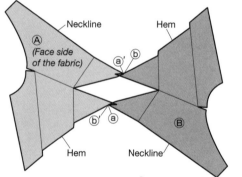

❹ Reverse the top and bottom of panel Ⓑ. Align point ⓑ of Ⓐ with point ⓐ' of Ⓑ, and point ⓐ of Ⓐ with point ⓑ' of Ⓑ.

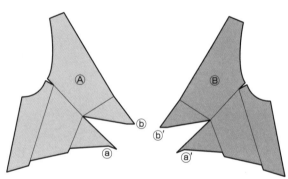

❺ Draw the neckline and the hemline in smooth, continuous lines. Join the bust points of panels Ⓐ and Ⓑ. Mark the shoulder line of Ⓑ as Ⓐ, and the hemline as Ⓑ.

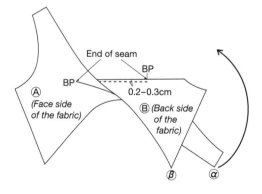

❻ Fold Ⓑ towards the front. Edge-stitch between the bust points to emphasize the crest of the fold when the fabric is twisted. Twist Ⓐ backwards. As it is twisted, the back side of panel Ⓑ appears on the front.

Flip turn for a draped effect

I increased the depth of the shadows by rotating the fabric and then flipping it over like the flip turn of swimmers in a pool.

Structure of the flip turn

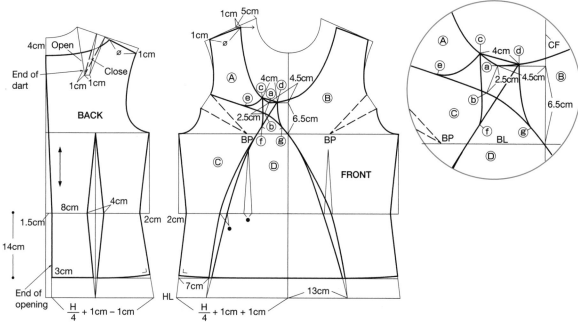

❶ Draft the pattern. Insert design lines in the bodice front pattern before making gathers. Firstly, mark panels Ⓐ and Ⓑ and then draw panels Ⓒ and Ⓓ to extend along the length of Ⓐ and Ⓑ in any way you want, as if you were drawing a picture. Insert waist darts in the design lines.

❷ The picture shows how Ⓒ is flipped over and connected to Ⓓ.

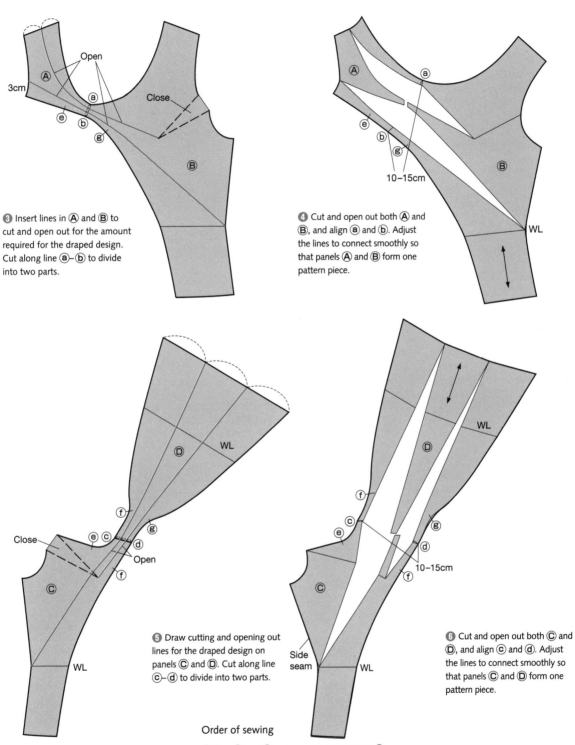

3 Insert lines in (A) and (B) to cut and open out for the amount required for the draped design. Cut along line (a)–(b) to divide into two parts.

4 Cut and open out both (A) and (B), and align (a) and (b). Adjust the lines to connect smoothly so that panels (A) and (B) form one pattern piece.

5 Draw cutting and opening out lines for the draped design on panels (C) and (D). Cut along line (c)–(d) to divide into two parts.

6 Cut and open out both (C) and (D), and align (c) and (d). Adjust the lines to connect smoothly so that panels (C) and (D) form one pattern piece.

Order of sewing

1 Sew (A) and (C) as far as the end of seam (e).

2 Twist panel (D) at (c)–(d), and sew panels (C) and (D) as far as end of seam (f). The underside of panel (D) will appear on the top.

3 Sew (B) and (D) as far as the end of seam (g).

● As the underside of section (D) will appear on top, be careful about your choice of fabric.

Page 56: Flip turn

A "flip turn" draped-design tie appears from the slit in the front bodice for a complex and beautiful effect.

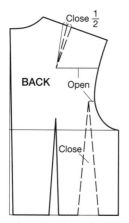

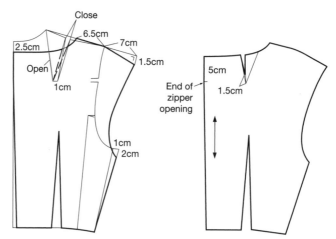

1 Draft a pattern for the bodice back.

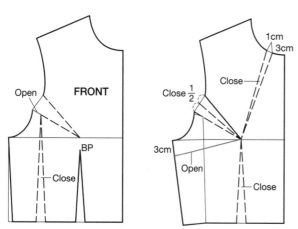

2 Draft a pattern for the bodice front. As the design has a very open neckline, close any excess in the front neckline and add to the side darts.

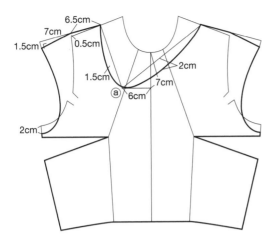

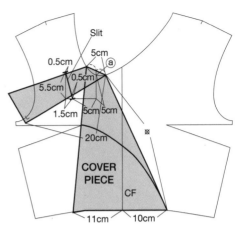

❸ Close all the darts. Draw the line of the asymmetrical neckline. Mark the deepest part of the neckline ⓐ.

❹ Draw the pattern for the tie from the waist towards the neckline and determine the position of the slit. Draw so that the tie fits well into the slit when turned at the neckline. Draw a design line for the bodice in a position that is concealed by the tie.

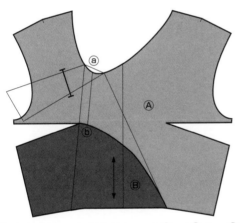

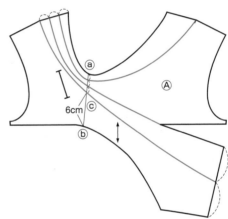

❺ The bodice front is divided into panels Ⓐ and Ⓑ. From ⓐ on panel Ⓐ, draw line ⓐ–ⓑ parallel to the edge of the tie.

❻ Mark ⓒ 6cm above ⓑ. Divide the area between ⓐ and ⓒ into three equal sections, and draw the cutting and opening out lines of the draped section, avoiding the position of the slit.

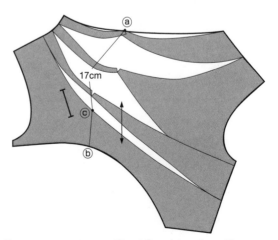

❼ Open out 17cm between ⓐ and ⓒ, and draw the neckline.

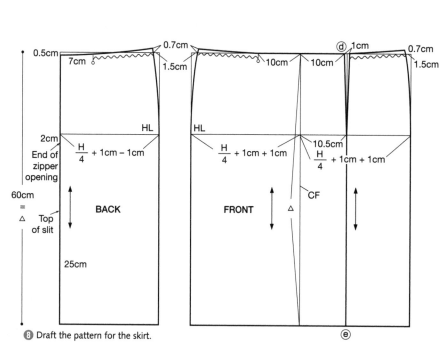

0.5cm   7cm   0.7cm   0.7cm   ⓓ 1cm   0.7cm

1.5cm   10cm   10cm   1.5cm

HL   HL

2cm
End of
zipper
opening $\dfrac{H}{4} + 1cm - 1cm$ $\dfrac{H}{4} + 1cm + 1cm$ 10.5cm $\dfrac{H}{4} + 1cm + 1cm$

60cm
=
△   Top
of slit   **BACK**   **FRONT**   CF   △

25cm   ⓔ

8 Draft the pattern for the skirt.

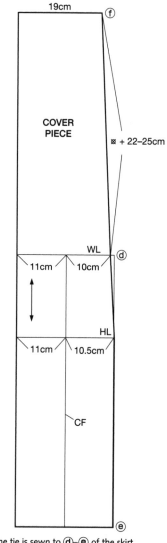

19cm   ⓕ

**COVER
PIECE**

⊠ + 22–25cm

WL   ⓓ
11cm   10cm

HL
11cm   10.5cm

CF

ⓔ

9 As the tie is sewn to ⓓ–ⓔ of the skirt
front, draft the pattern with the skirt pattern
as a base. It is structured to separate from the
bodice at the waistline, to turn at the neckline
and emerge from the slit. Add 22–25cm to
the measurement ⊠ in **4** for the length of
the tie above the waistline.

Different facings, different looks

Attaching a variety of neckline facings to a similar-shaped bodice gives a range of options. These invisible facings give each garment an individual shape.

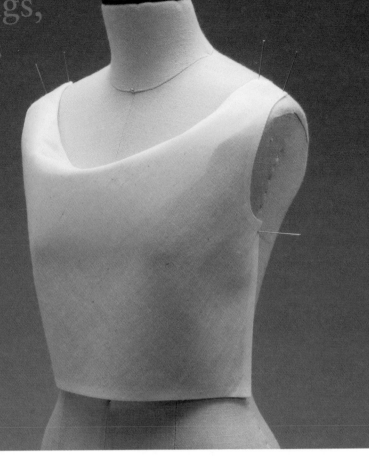

Basic bodice front

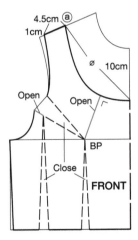

4.5cm ⓐ
1cm
ø 10cm
Open   Open
BP
Close
FRONT

❶ Draft a pattern for the bodice front. Draw a round neckline and then draw a cutting and opening out line from the bust point at a right angle to the neckline. Mark the neckline measurement ø.

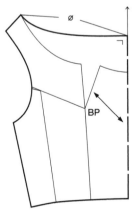

ø
BP

❷ Close all the darts and open at the neckline. Extend the neckline to the line that extends upwards from the centre front till it becomes measurement ø. To achieve a soft look, make the grain on the centre front on the bias.

The facing is a curve

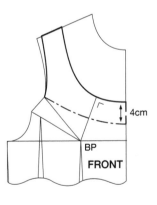

4cm
BP
FRONT

Draw the facing on the neckline of the bodice before you cut and open it.

The facing is square

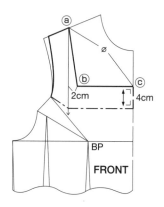

Draw a square neckline. Make ⓐ–ⓑ–ⓒ into ∅ measurement.

The facing is V-shaped

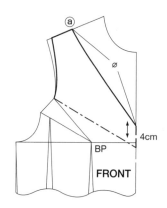

Draw a V-shaped neckline that measures ∅ from ⓐ.

The facing is asymmetrical

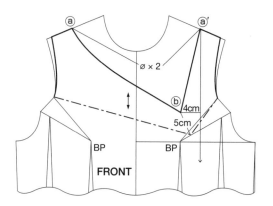

Draw an asymmetrical neckline. Determine point ⓑ and make ⓐ–ⓑ–ⓐ' into ∅ × 2.
As the neckline on the bodice is stretched at ⓑ, the fabric on the bodice left and right
appears to be intersecting at the neckline.

Page 57: Different facings, different looks

A gentle, asymmetrical drape of the neckline and the hemline which recalls the elegance of a bygone age.

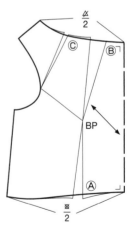

Because the shape of the neckline and the hemline changes according to the facing, draft the pattern for the outer fabric after deciding on the facing, to make the garment easier to shape.

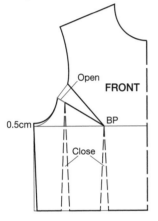

① Draft the pattern for the bodice front. Move all the waist darts to the armhole darts.

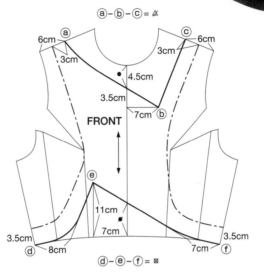

ⓐ–ⓑ–ⓒ = ⚠

6cm
3cm
ⓒ 6cm
3cm
● 4.5cm
3.5cm
7cm ⓑ

FRONT

ⓔ
11cm
7cm ●
3.5cm
ⓓ 8cm
7cm ⓕ
3.5cm

ⓓ–ⓔ–ⓕ = ⊠

② Draw the asymmetrical neckline and mark the ⓐ–ⓑ–ⓒ neckline measurement as ⚠. So that the fabric appears to be layered, draw the hemline in reverse asymmetry to the neckline. Make the ⓓ–ⓔ–ⓕ neckline measurement ⊠.

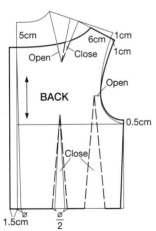

③ Draft the pattern for the bodice back. Move the shoulder darts to the neckline. (The facing for the bodice back is omitted.)

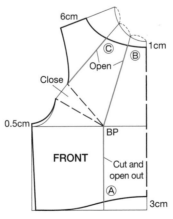

6cm
ⓒ ⓑ 1cm
Open
Close
0.5cm
FRONT
BP
Cut and open out
Ⓐ
3cm

④ Draft the pattern for the bodice front. Trim 1cm off the neckline and 3cm at the hem along the centre front. When you do this, make sure that the neckline and hem measurements are not more than the ● and ✦ measurements in ②, respectively. The larger the difference, the greater the overlapping of fabric in the completed garment.

⚠/2
ⓒ ⓑ
BP
Ⓐ
⊠/2

⑤ Close the armhole darts and cut and open out at Ⓐ so that the hemline measurement becomes ⊠/2. Close the remaining armhole darts and cut and open out at Ⓑ. Next cut and open out again at ⓒ so that the neckline measurement becomes ⚠/2. Draw the neckline and the hemline.

Page 58: Cowl neck

The fabric flows softly from both shoulders.

From the side, it appears that the drape is protruding from the fitted bodice.

The cowl neck is said to have originated in the high priest's robe of the Middle Ages.
Here it is incorporated into an elegant dress.

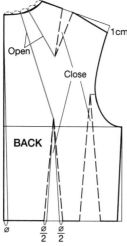

❶ Draft a pattern for the draped design. As the draped design is created at the neckline, close all the darts and open out at the neckline.

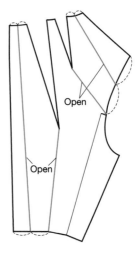

❷ Add cutting and opening out lines on the neckline.

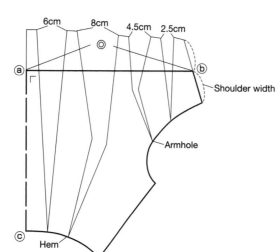

❸ Cut and open out more at the centre than close to the shoulder line. Measure the shoulder width and mark ⓑ. Draw a line from ⓑ to meet the centre back line at a right angle and mark ⓓ. ⓐ–ⓑ becomes the back neckline.

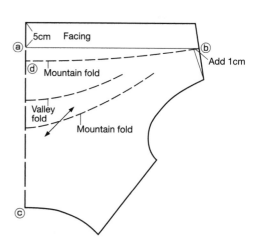

❹ On the pattern in ❸, add 5cm for the facing above the neckline ⓐ–ⓑ and roughly cut out the fabric. When you put the garment on a dress form, the fabric will naturally drape, bringing the fold line lower to ⓓ–ⓑ. A second mountain fold will also appear as the neckline settles into position.

Page 59: Application of the cowl-neck design

Seen from the side the silhouette, with its gently opening neckline, echoes the opening petals of a flower.

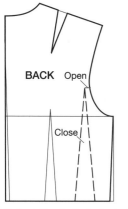

① Draft a pattern for the bodice back.

BACK Open Close

0.5cm 1cm ∅ ∅/2

② Draw the very wide, open front neckline.

FRONT 0.5cm Open Open Close BP 5cm 6.5cm 3cm 1.5cm

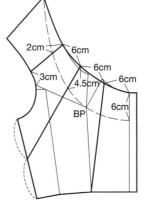

③ Close all the darts and open at the neckline. On the inside of the neckline, draw a large curve that passes through the bust point with a dashed line. This dashed line is the position where the neckline will start to open out, just like the petals of a flower.

2cm 6cm 3cm 6cm 6cm 4.5cm BP 6cm

④ Open out the neckline at the points where design lines and the dashed lines intersect.

0.5cm 0.5cm 0.7cm 0.7cm 1cm 1cm Base point

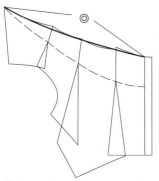

⑤ Connect the pattern pieces and redraw the neckline.

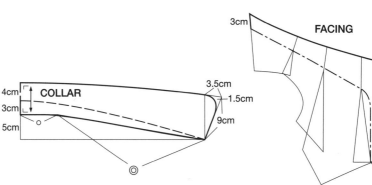

⑥ Draft a pattern for the collar.

COLLAR 4cm 3cm 5cm 3.5cm 1.5cm 9cm

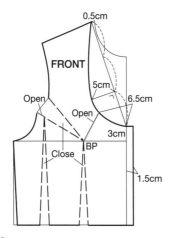

FACING 3cm 6cm

Page 60: Application of the cowl-neck design

The draped design is created by cutting and opening out a large amount of the neckline. By opening it out only a little, I tried to create a shirt with a silhouette that looks like the pout of a pigeon.
It is even more effective when you make it with a firm fabric.

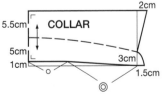

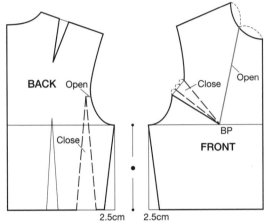

❶ Draft a pattern. Close ⅔ of the armhole darts and open at the neckline. Make the remaining ⅓ into darts.

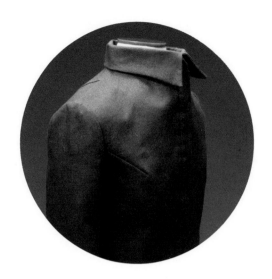

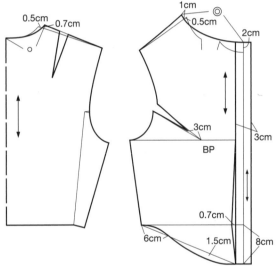

❷ As wrinkles will form when you put on the shirt, add additional room in the front and back neckline.

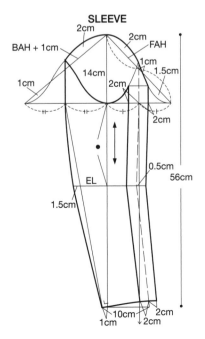

❸ Draft patterns for the collar and the sleeve. To achieve a balance with the unique bodice design, make the sleeves slim and slightly longer.

Part 3
It vanished ...

Pattern Magic!

I thought it would be interesting to see

if I could make part of the garment disappear

by manipulating the pattern.

Not a trick of the eye like *trompe l'oeil*,

but achieved by skilfully blending concept and pattern.

A vanishing scarf (See page 90 for instructions)

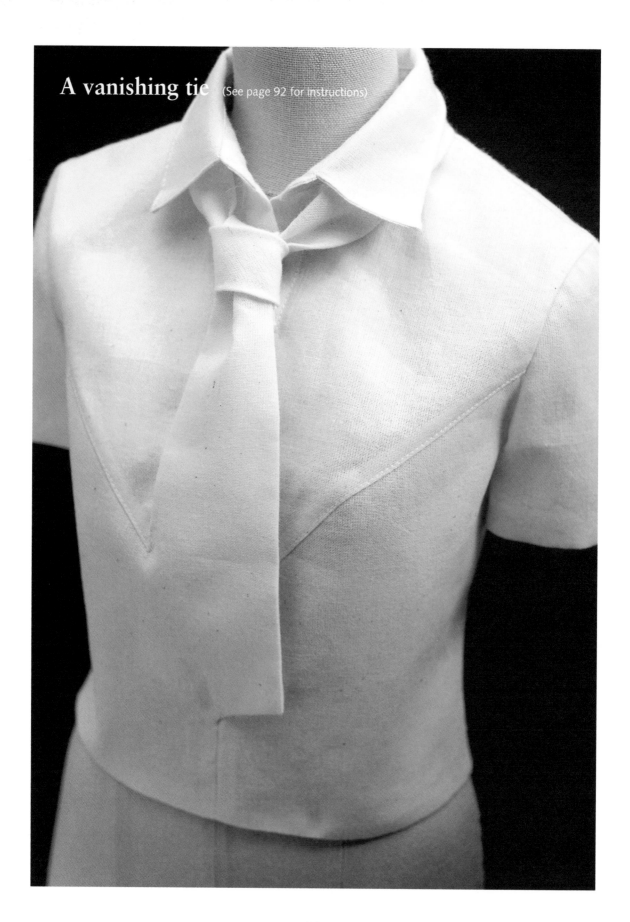

A vanishing tie (See page 92 for instructions)

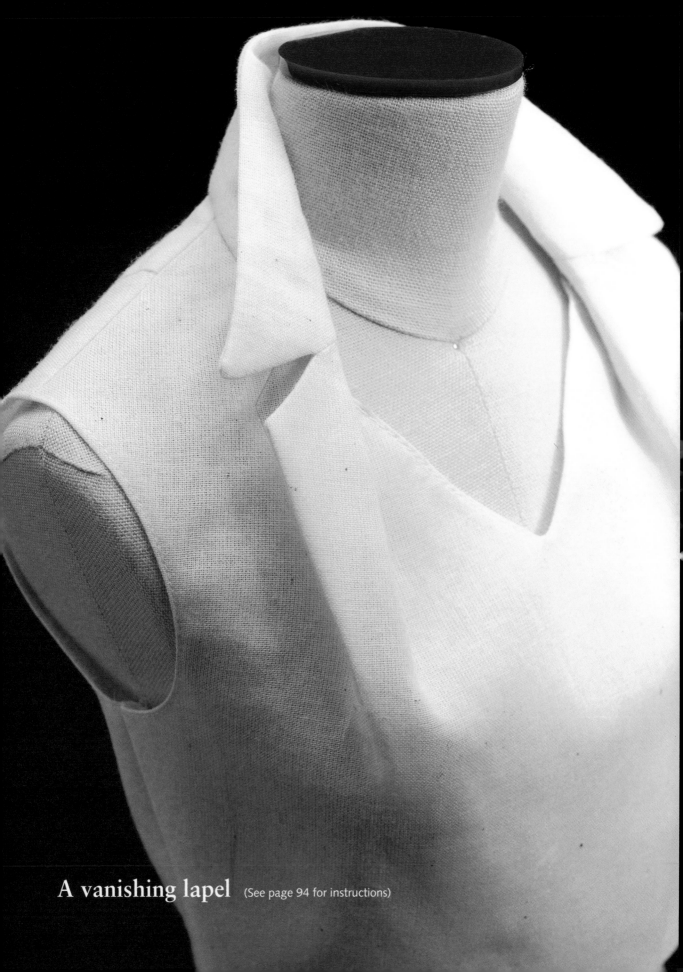

A vanishing lapel (See page 94 for instructions)

A vanishing pocket (See pages 96 and 97 for instructions)

A

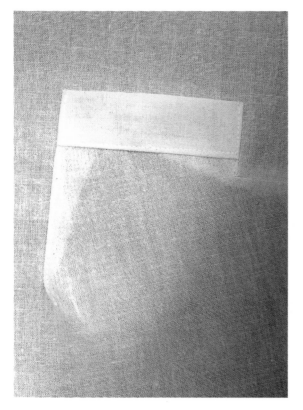

B

Make a pattern …
for a part of the garment
that "vanishes"

Page 85: A vanishing scarf

The scarf wound around the neck
becomes part of the bodice,
and disappears!

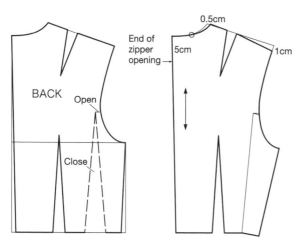

❶ Draft the pattern. Close the darts on the bodice back that are towards the side seams.

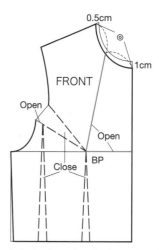

❷ On the bodice front, close the darts on both the bust line and the neckline and cut and open out.

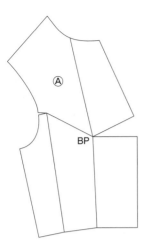

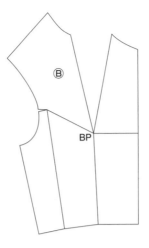

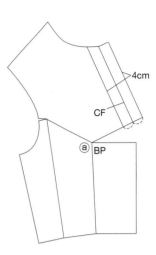

4cm

CF

ⓐ BP

3 Mark the pattern that is cut and opened out at the bust line as Ⓐ and the pattern that is cut and opened out at the neckline as Ⓑ.

4 Attach the placket above the bust line on pattern Ⓐ. Mark the bust point ⓐ.

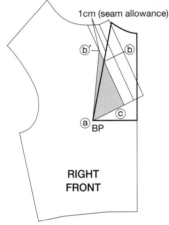

1cm (seam allowance)

ⓑ' ⓑ

ⓐ ⓒ
BP

RIGHT FRONT

5 Draft the pattern for the top bodice front. Place pattern Ⓑ on top of the pattern in **4**. Ⓑ is the part of the bodice of which the scarf becomes a part and then disappears. As overlapping of the bodice and scarf will not take place when the scarf is attached, cut out the overlapping portion and the placket as two separate pieces. The triangular section ⓐ ⓑ and ⓒ is the overlapping portion. As seam allowances are necessary for sewing the side of the triangle ⓐ–ⓑ to the bodice, add 1cm, and move ⓑ to ⓑ'. Cut out ⓐ ⓑ' ⓒ separately.

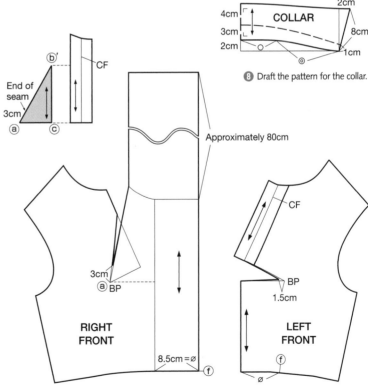

ⓑ'
CF

End of seam
3cm

ⓐ ⓒ

Approximately 80cm

3cm
ⓐ BP

RIGHT FRONT

8.5cm = ∅
ⓕ

6 Pattern after connecting the scarf and bodice.

| 2cm |
4cm	**COLLAR**	
3cm		8cm
2cm	◯	1cm
	◎	

8 Draft the pattern for the collar.

CF

BP
1.5cm

ⓕ

∅

LEFT FRONT

7 For the lower bodice front, use the bodice in **4**. Make the darts shorter so that they are concealed by the scarf.

91

Page 86: A vanishing tie

By clever design the point of the tie disappears into the shirt.

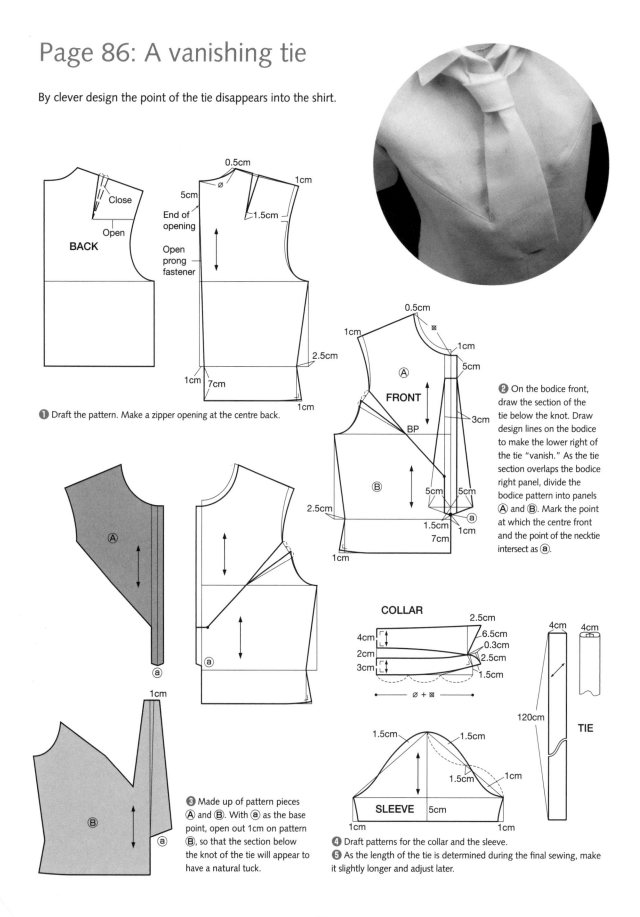

BACK

Close
Open

0.5cm
∅
5cm
End of opening
1cm
1.5cm
Open prong fastener
2.5cm
1cm
7cm
1cm

❶ Draft the pattern. Make a zipper opening at the centre back.

0.5cm
⊠
1cm
1cm
5cm
Ⓐ
FRONT
3cm
BP
Ⓑ
2.5cm
5cm 5cm
ⓐ
1.5cm 1cm
7cm
1cm

❷ On the bodice front, draw the section of the tie below the knot. Draw design lines on the bodice to make the lower right of the tie "vanish." As the tie section overlaps the bodice right panel, divide the bodice pattern into panels Ⓐ and Ⓑ. Mark the point at which the centre front and the point of the necktie intersect as ⓐ.

Ⓐ
ⓐ
1cm
Ⓑ
ⓐ

❸ Made up of pattern pieces Ⓐ and Ⓑ. With ⓐ as the base point, open out 1cm on pattern Ⓑ, so that the section below the knot of the tie will appear to have a natural tuck.

COLLAR
2.5cm
4cm
6.5cm
0.3cm
2cm
2.5cm
3cm
1.5cm
∅ + ⊠

4cm 4cm

120cm

TIE

SLEEVE
1.5cm 1.5cm
1.5cm 1cm
5cm
1cm 1cm

❹ Draft patterns for the collar and the sleeve.
❺ As the length of the tie is determined during the final sewing, make it slightly longer and adjust later.

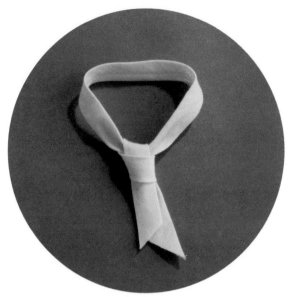

6 Tie the tie.

7 Place the bodice on a dress form and attach the tie. Decide where you want to position the knot in the tie but leave enough room for the wearer's head to fit through.

8 Once you've decided on the position of the knot, cut off the section below the knot. What you have cut off the tie will not be needed.

9 Attach the top section of the tie to the collar, and insert the tie for bodice panel **Ⓑ** into the knot. Arrange the tie so that it looks natural, and hem in such a way as not to be noticeable.

Page 87: A vanishing lapel

The lapels of this tailored collar fade into the garment.

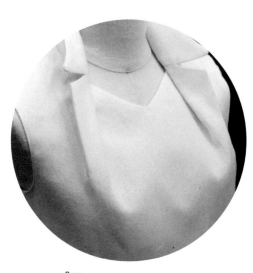

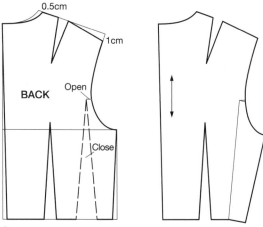

0.5cm

1cm

BACK

Open

Close

1 Draft the pattern. Close the darts on the bodice back, that are towards the side seams.

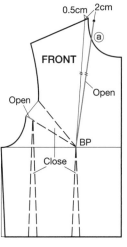

0.5cm 2cm

ⓐ

FRONT

Open

Open

BP

Close

2 Draw the cutting and opening out line and mark the point at which the neckline and the cutting and opening out line intersect as ⓐ.

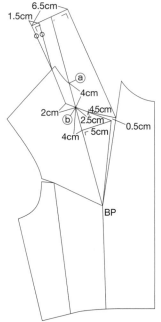

6.5cm
1.5cm
ⓐ
4cm
2cm 4.5cm
ⓑ 2.5cm
4cm 5cm 0.5cm
BP

3 Close the darts and draft the pattern for the tailored collar. Mark the position at which the lapel starts ⓑ.

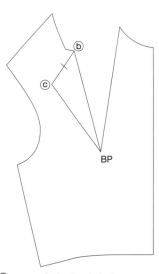

ⓑ
ⓒ
BP

4 Reverse the lapel with the line connecting ⓑ and the bust point as an axis, and copy. Mark the point of the lapel ⓒ.

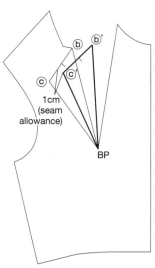

ⓑ ⓑ'
ⓒ ⓒ'
1cm
(seam
allowance)
BP

5 Measure the seam allowance of the lapel. With the bust point as the pivotal point, move the point of the lapel to the position where it opens out by 1cm, and mark the points ⓒ' and ⓑ'.

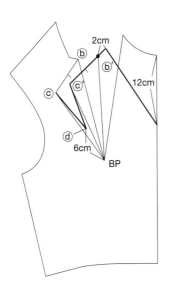

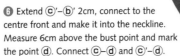

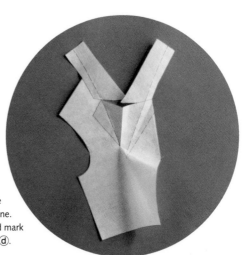

6 Extend ⓒ'–ⓑ' 2cm, connect to the centre front and make it into the neckline. Measure 6cm above the bust point and mark the point ⓓ. Connect ⓒ–ⓓ and ⓒ'–ⓓ.

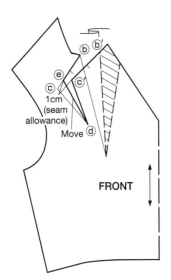

FRONT

7 So that the design lines of the bodice are not obvious, leave only about 1cm for the seam allowance and move ⓒ–ⓓ to ⓔ–ⓓ.

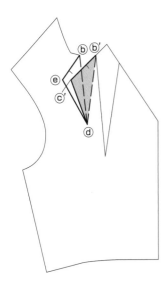

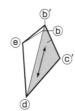

8 Reverse the triangle formed from ⓑ'–ⓒ'–ⓓ. Align ⓑ–ⓓ–ⓔ along the line ⓑ'–ⓓ. As lines ⓑ'–ⓓ and ⓑ–ⓓ are of different lengths, draw a line connecting ⓑ' and ⓔ. The rhombus shape made from ⓑ'–ⓔ–ⓓ–ⓒ' is the part that is concealed in the lapel.

Make any sections that are difficult to understand in the drawing from notepaper first, in order to make them easier to understand.

Page 88: A vanishing pocket A

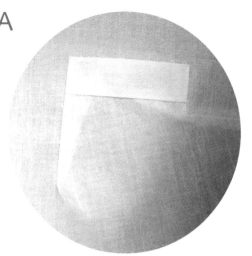

The pocket disappears into the garment
like a half-drawn picture.

The same advanced technique of closing darts
and opening out is applied here.

Pockets A, B, and C are decorative, not functional.

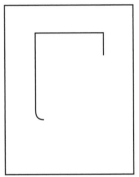

❶ Draw the outline of the pocket, and with
an eraser rub out the places where you want
the corners of the pockets to "disappear."

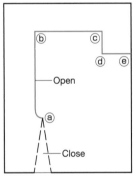

❷ When fitting the pocket to a three-
dimensional dress form, you can use darts to
delete the design lines. Make ⓐ the point
where the dart ends, and try making the
pocket with just one of the design lines ⓓ–ⓔ.

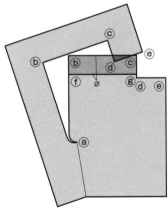

❸ When the darts are closed, the base and
the pattern overlap. Make a design line in the
pocket opening. I made it measurement ⌀,
considering the amount for the seam allowance
and a balanced position for the design line.

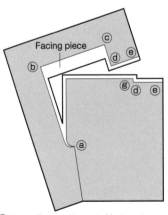

❹ Seam allowance is created by inserting a
design line into the pocket opening.

❺ Add seam allowance to the design line.
As the area around the pocket opening on
the base (the base fabric below ⓑ–ⓒ)
serves as the pocket facing piece, make it as
large as possible.

Page 88: A vanishing pocket B

Just as a sinking boat disappears beneath the water,
the left corner of the pocket seems to sink and vanish.

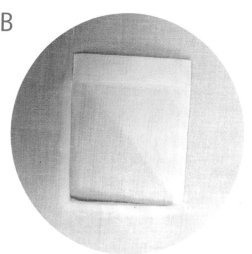

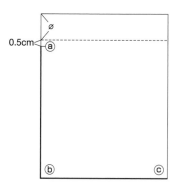

❶ Decide where you want the pocket to "vanish"
ⓐ–ⓑ–ⓒ.

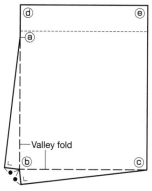

❷ With ⓑ as the pivotal point, decide the depth to
which the corner of the pocket is to sink (●) and connect
at right angles with ⓐ and ⓒ. ⓐ–ⓑ–ⓒ will be a
valley fold.

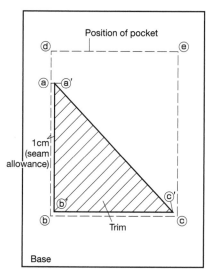

❸ Add seam allowance to the pocket attachment
position ⓐ–ⓑ–ⓒ of the base fabric. As the triangle
surrounded by ⓐ'–ⓑ'–ⓒ' is unnecessary, trim it.

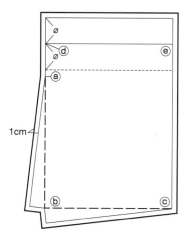

❹ To the pocket pattern add the amount required
for folding back the pocket opening, and the seam
allowance.

Page 88: A vanishing pocket C

The corner of the pocket seems to vanish into the bodice.

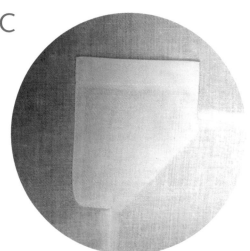

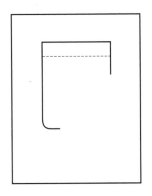

❶ Draw the outline of the pocket and with an eraser rub out the places where you want the corners of the pockets to "disappear."

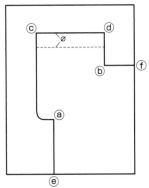

❷ From points ⓐ and ⓑ, draw design lines ⓐ–ⓔ and ⓑ–ⓕ. As long as they pass through points ⓐ and ⓑ, you can position points ⓔ and ⓕ anywhere.

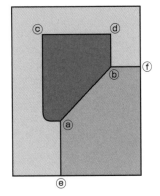

❸ Make two patterns, with the area surrounded by ⓐ–ⓑ–ⓓ–ⓒ duplicated on the base fabric and the pocket.

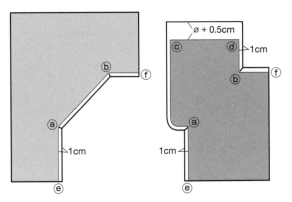

❹ Add seam allowance to the base fabric and the pocket.

The basis for pattern development is the

Bunka-style sloper (block) for an adult woman

The Bunka-style sloper (block), created for the body shape of the modern Japanese women, is constructed three-dimensionally and fitted to the body with darts (bust darts, back shoulder darts, waist darts).

Bust (B), waist (W) and centre-back (CB) length measurements are required to draw the sloper (block). The measurements for each part of the body are based on the bust measurement, and the size of each dart has been calculated from the bust and waist measurements. Each waist dart is calculated by the formula—bodice − (W/2 + 3)—where 3cm is the amount of ease added. Precise calculations are required for a neat fit, but drawings will be relatively easy if you refer to the quick reference table of measurements for each part of the body. Pages 102 and 103 feature half-scale slopers for each of the bust sizes (77, 80, 83, 86 and 89cm) for you to use.

Quick reference table of measurements for different parts of the body

(Unit: cm)

B	Body width $\frac{B}{2}+6$	Ⓐ – BL $\frac{B}{12}+13.7$	Back width $\frac{B}{8}+7.4$	BL – Ⓑ $\frac{B}{5}+8.3$	Chest width $\frac{B}{8}+6.2$	$\frac{B}{32}$ $\frac{B}{32}$	Front neckline width $\frac{B}{24}+3.4=◎$	Front neckline depth $◎+0.5$	Bust darts $(\frac{B}{4}-2.5)°$	Back neckline width $◎+0.2$	Back shoulder darts $\frac{B}{32}-0.8$
77	44.5	20.1	17.0	23.7	15.8	2.4	6.6	7.1	16.8	6.8	1.6
78	45.0	20.2	17.2	23.9	16.0	2.4	6.7	7.2	17.0	6.9	1.6
79	45.5	20.3	17.3	24.1	16.1	2.5	6.7	7.2	17.3	6.9	1.7
80	46.0	20.4	17.4	24.3	16.2	2.5	6.7	7.2	17.5	6.9	1.7
81	46.5	20.5	17.5	24.5	16.3	2.5	6.8	7.3	17.8	7.0	1.7
82	47.0	20.5	17.7	24.7	16.5	2.6	6.8	7.3	18.0	7.0	1.8
83	47.5	20.6	17.8	24.9	16.6	2.6	6.9	7.4	18.3	7.1	1.8
84	48.0	20.7	17.9	25.1	16.7	2.6	6.9	7.4	18.5	7.1	1.8
85	48.5	20.8	18.0	25.3	16.8	2.7	6.9	7.4	18.8	7.1	1.9
86	49.0	20.9	18.2	25.5	17.0	2.7	7.0	7.5	19.0	7.2	1.9
87	49.5	21.0	18.3	25.7	17.1	2.7	7.0	7.5	19.3	7.2	1.9
88	50.0	21.0	18.4	25.9	17.2	2.8	7.1	7.6	19.5	7.3	2.0
89	50.5	21.1	18.5	26.1	17.3	2.8	7.1	7.6	19.8	7.3	2.0

Waist dart measurement—Quick reference table

(Unit: cm)

Total darts volume 100%	f 7%	e 18%	d 35%	c 11%	b 15%	a 14%
9	0.6	1.6	3.1	1	1.4	1.3
10	0.7	1.8	3.5	1.1	1.5	1.4
11	0.8	2	3.9	1.2	1.6	1.5
12	0.8	2.2	4.2	1.3	1.8	1.7
12.5	0.9	2.3	4.3	1.3	1.9	1.8

Making a drawing of a sloper (block)

Slopers (blocks) are made for both the bodice and the sleeve, but only the method of drawing a bodice sloper (block), used throughout this book, is explained here.

Basic lines

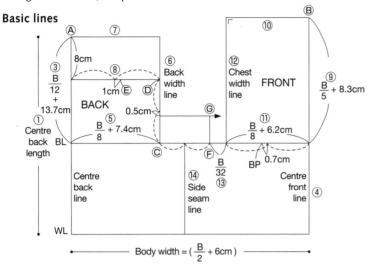

Firstly draw the basic lines for the bodice. Accurately measure each part of the body and draw lines in the order of ① to ⑭. The numbers in the guide table are also arranged for reading from the left in order to help you proceed with pattern drafting in that order.

Curved lines

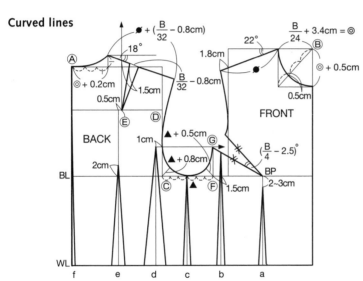

After drawing the basic lines, draw the curved lines of the neckline, shoulder, and armhole, and finally the darts.

Tips for moving darts

When you close the waist darts with ⓐ as the pivotal point, the armhole opens. As it is only a small amount, consider it as ease in the armhole. The waist darts on the sloper (block) are marked when used for pattern-drafting but have been omitted where not required.

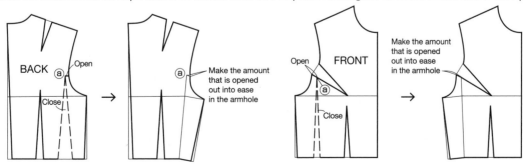

Bunka-style sloper (block) for an adult woman (Size M) (half-scale)

Copy at 200% on a photocopier to make the full-sized pattern.

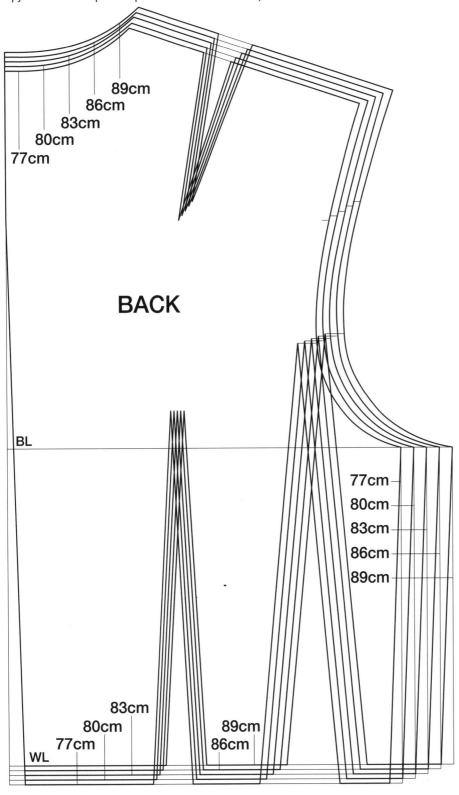

89cm
86cm
83cm
80cm
77cm

BACK

BL

77cm
80cm
83cm
86cm
89cm

83cm
80cm
77cm

89cm
86cm

WL

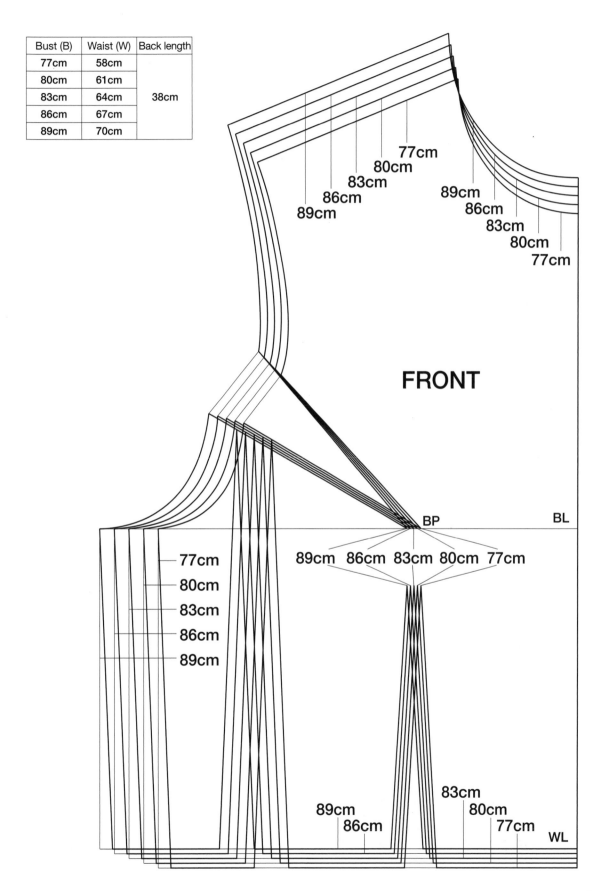

Bust (B)	Waist (W)	Back length
77cm	58cm	
80cm	61cm	
83cm	64cm	38cm
86cm	67cm	
89cm	70cm	

FRONT

In conclusion

One way to understand the makeup of clothing is to simply copy model pieces. One can easily discover the mechanisms behind any piece of clothing by using various means to copy it, then making a pattern from the recreated piece. When I copy a Dior garment, for example, I get a fleeting insight into his sense of fun. With patterns, there is always more than meets the eye, and giving shape to a garment after understanding the mechanisms at play is an even more profound experience. I hope this book will help you enjoy the process of pattern-making.

Finally, I would like to take this opportunity to offer my heartfelt gratitude to Mrs Fujino Kasai for the invaluable advice she gave me, as she did with my previous book, *Pattern Magic*, and to all the other people who helped make this book a reality.